A GALLERY OF BLIND DRAWINGS

A GALLERY OF BLIND DRAWINGS

Alison Touster-Reed

ISBN 9780991490790

Cordelia Hollis Publishing
McEwen, TN

PREFACE

I delight to share these drawings and their attending comments with new viewers and readers, just as I have shared them over the years, and continue to share new drawings, with family and friends. You will discover three components in the following pages: the drawings themselves, accompanying titles, and, dotted throughout the book, my comments on how these drawings came to be, what they mean to me, what they may come to mean to you. The comments are not meant to interpret the drawings with which they concur on the page but, rather, to speak more generally to the process of "blind drawing," as I have experienced it all my life. Let your reading and viewing of this work be a simple pleasure, as its creation has been for me.

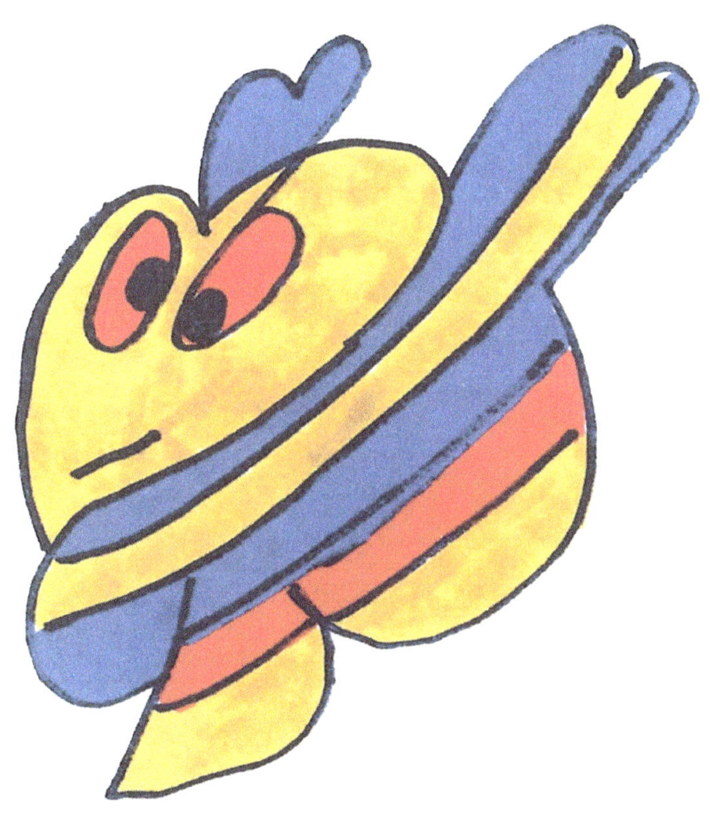

ANGRY BEE

I have been doing this sort of drawing virtually all my life, beginning, in a primitive fashion, in grammar school.

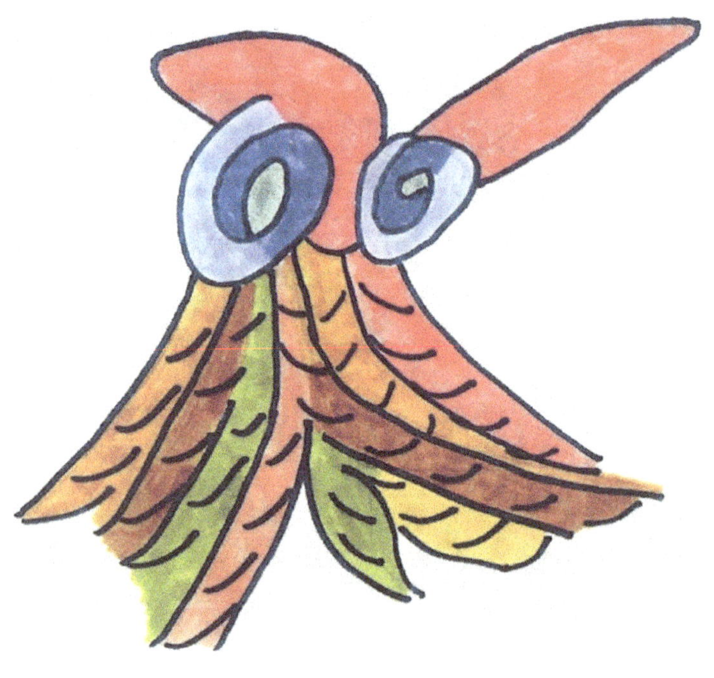

AUSTERE

I have become so accustomed to the experience of these drawings, an experience that I nevertheless cannot easily describe,

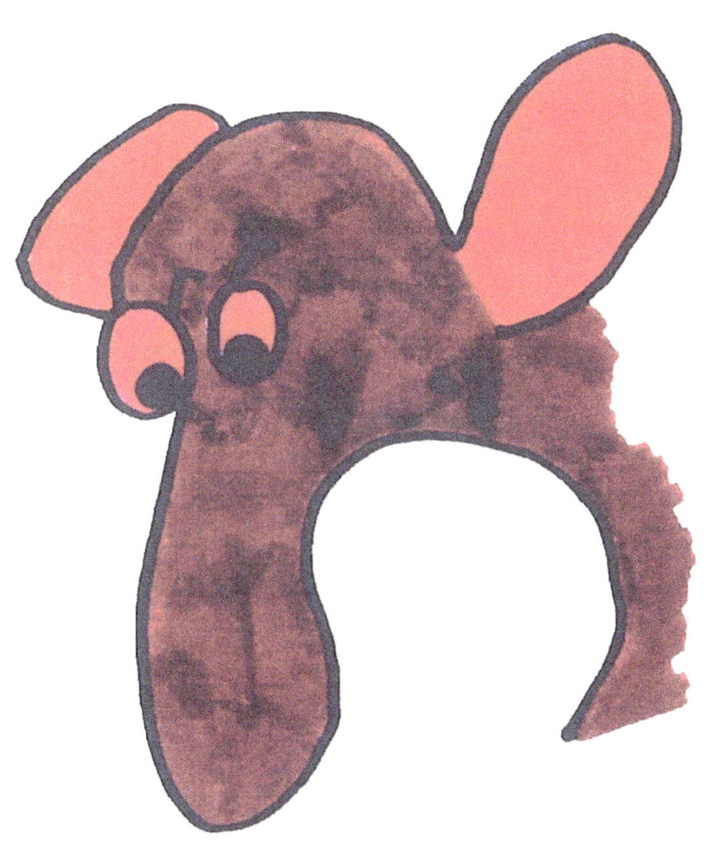

DISAPPROVAL

that the whole process of explanation at first seemed
impossible.

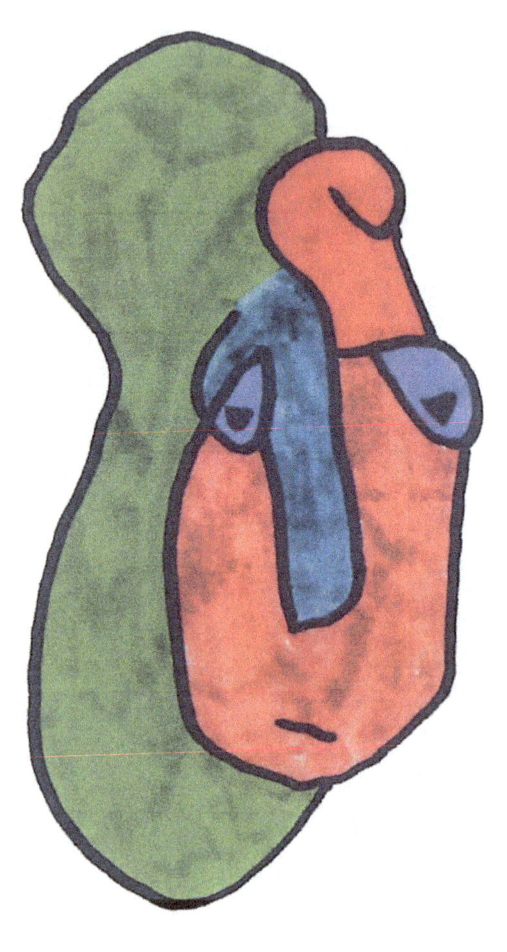

OH, WOE IS ME

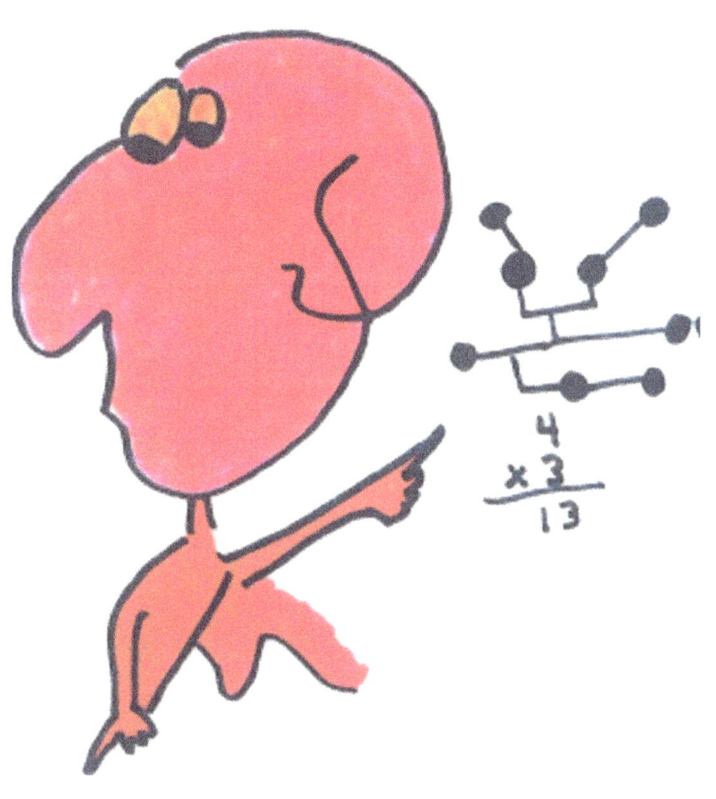

MATH PROFESSOR

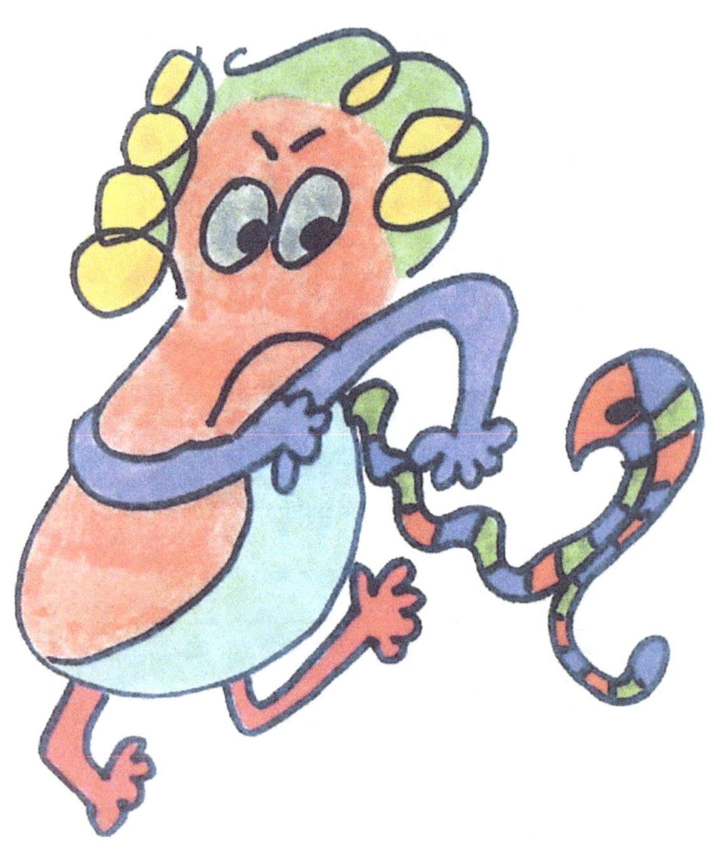

EVE

How can one helpfully describe a process or ritual that takes such a short time?

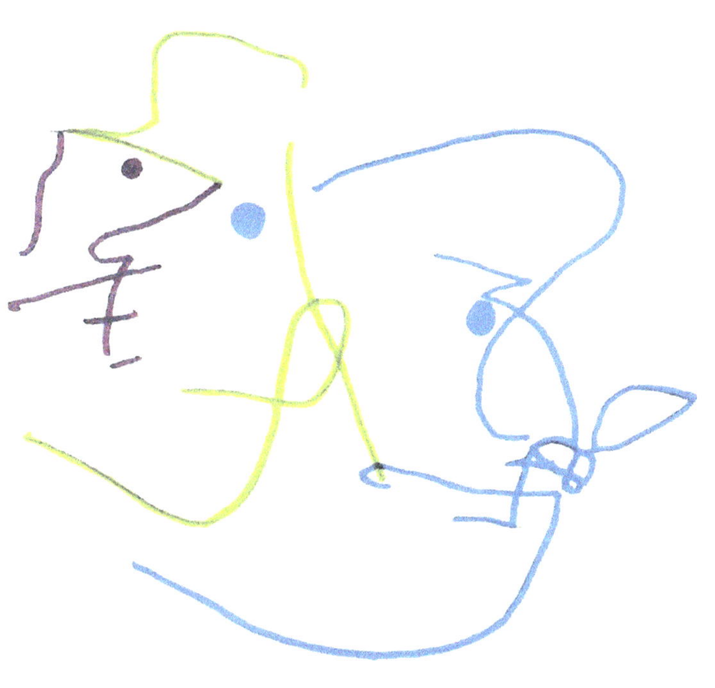

FACES

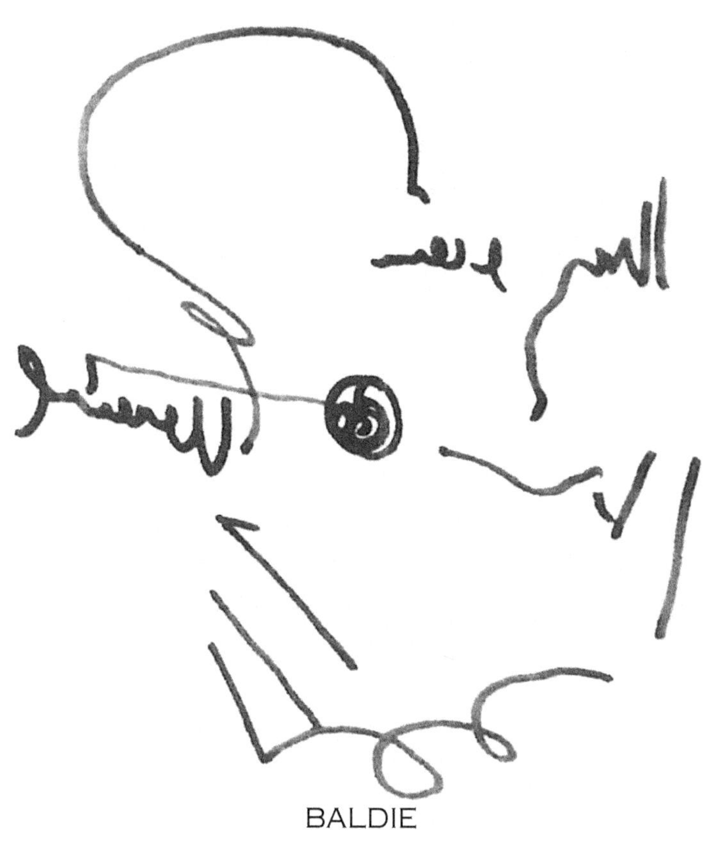

BALDIE

The process of drawing the initial images actually lasts only a matter of seconds.

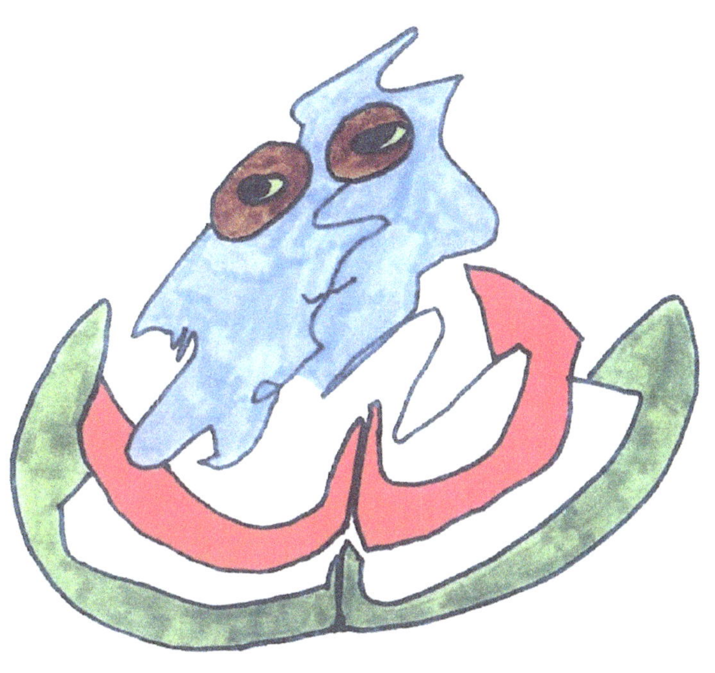

PRAYER

From the beginning my intent was serious and focused, not at all like doodling, and the experience brought pleasure to me.

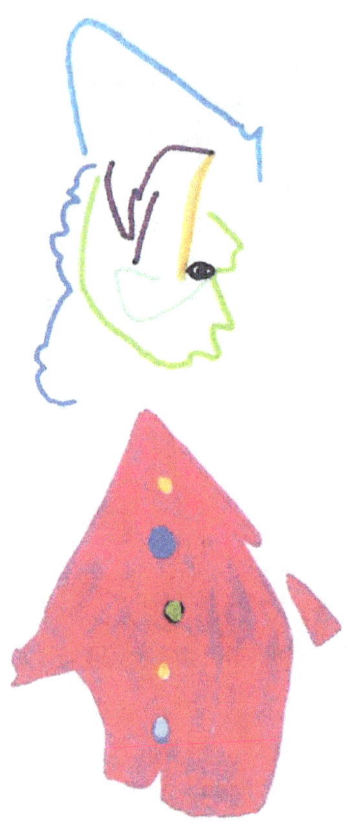

BABY CLOWN

The process is remarkably brief—

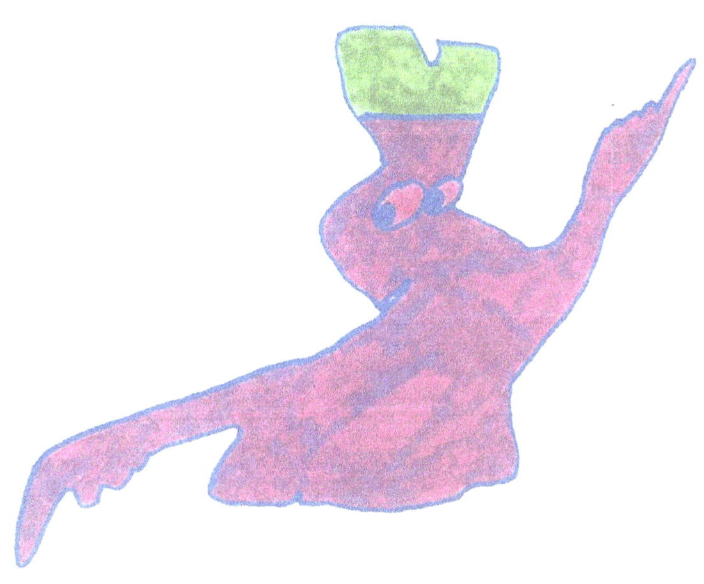

NEITHER HERE NOR THERE

so brief, in fact, that my editor and I actually considered calling the drawings "epiphanies," but that's a term carrying with it a spiritual con-notation I do not intend.

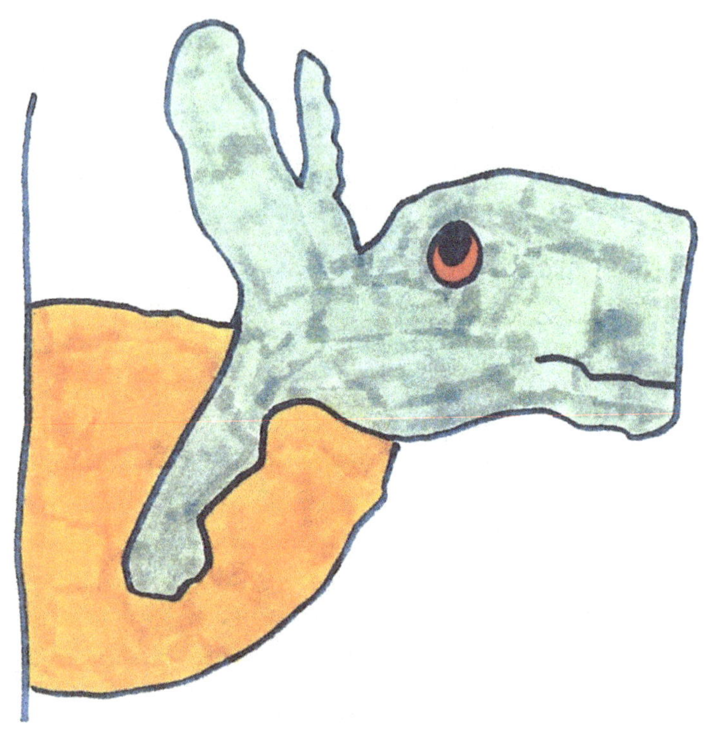

TROPHY

Each drawing comes to mind in something like a flash.

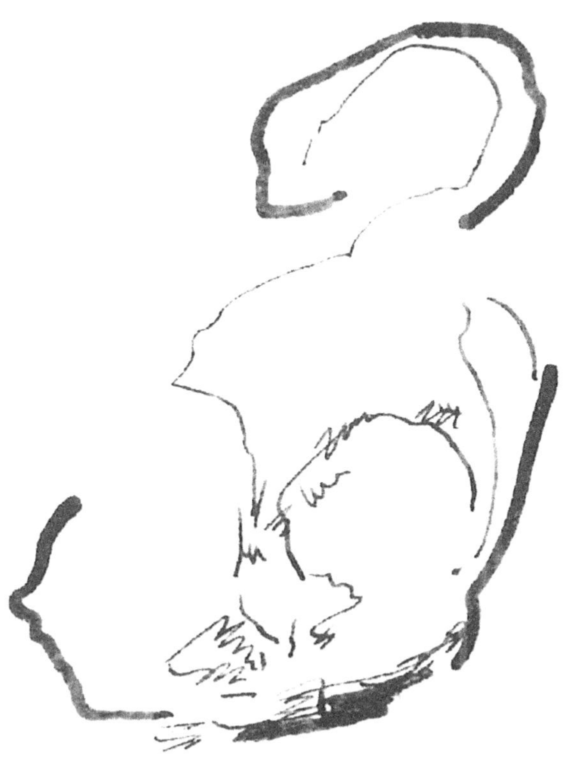

EMBEDDED

My hand expresses or draws the image instantly, even "blindly," without the governance of careful eye toward matters of composition.

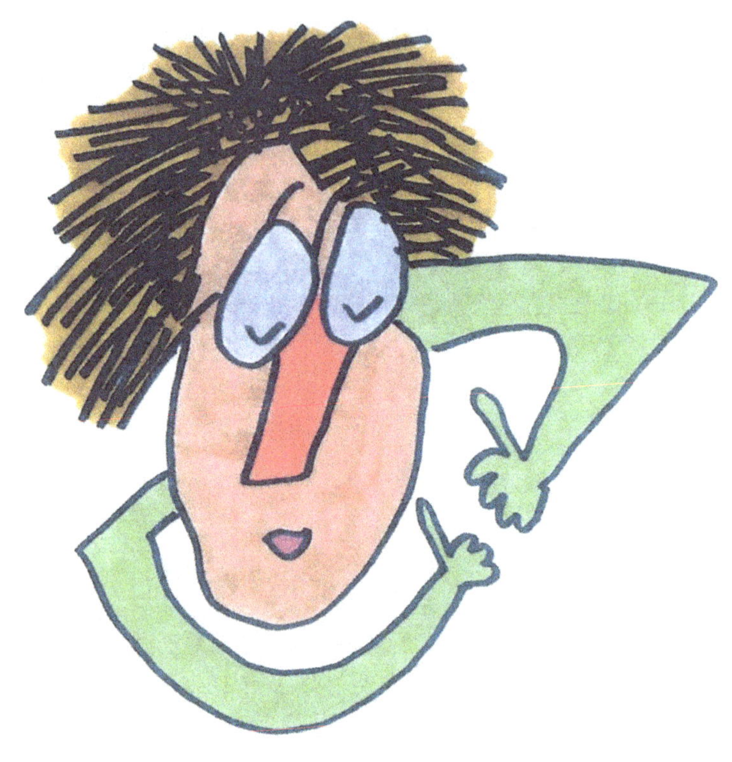

I began all these drawings with my eyes closed and a few with my left hand (even though I'm right-handed).

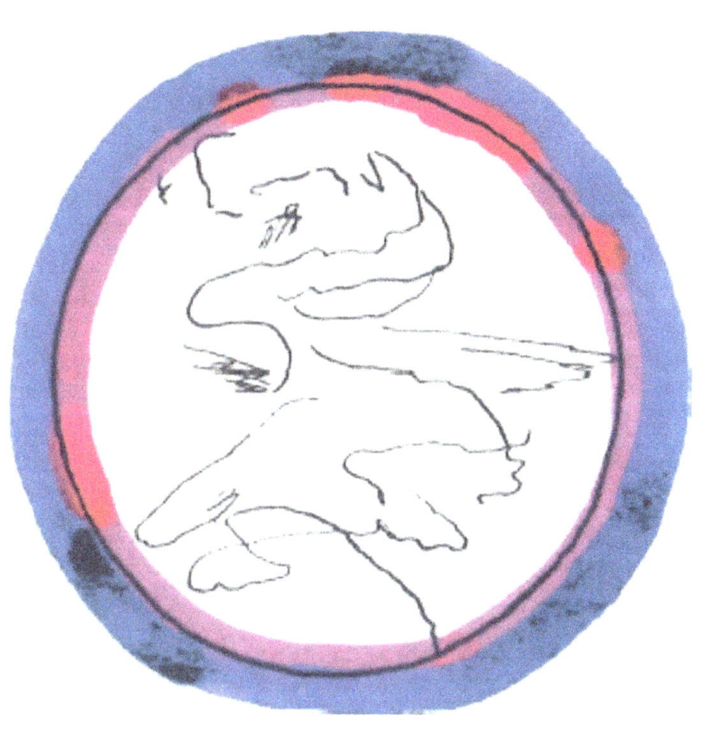

IN TUTU

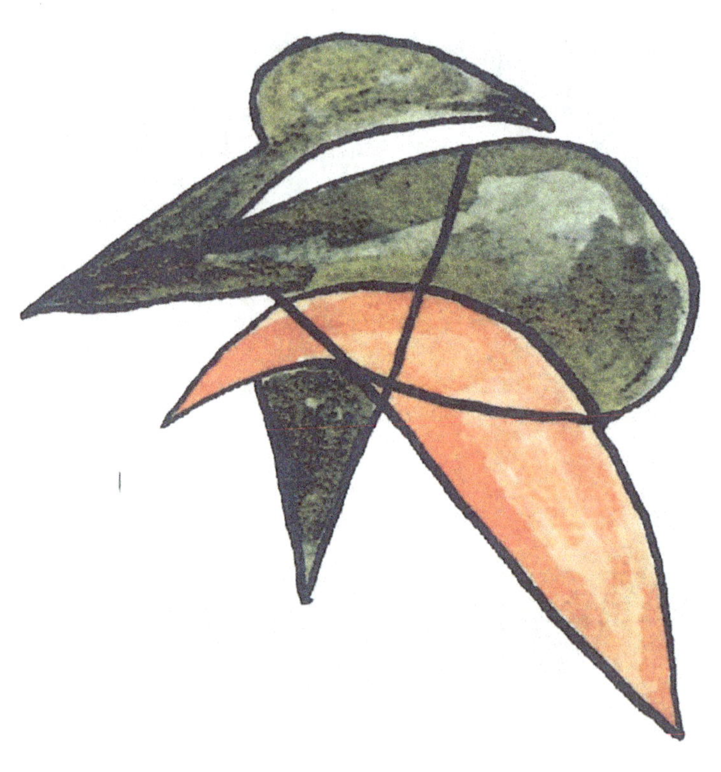

MOUSE AND BANANA

The process continues simply. I put the pencil to paper and pull it back or forward or in broken figures, according to the way my feeling dictates.

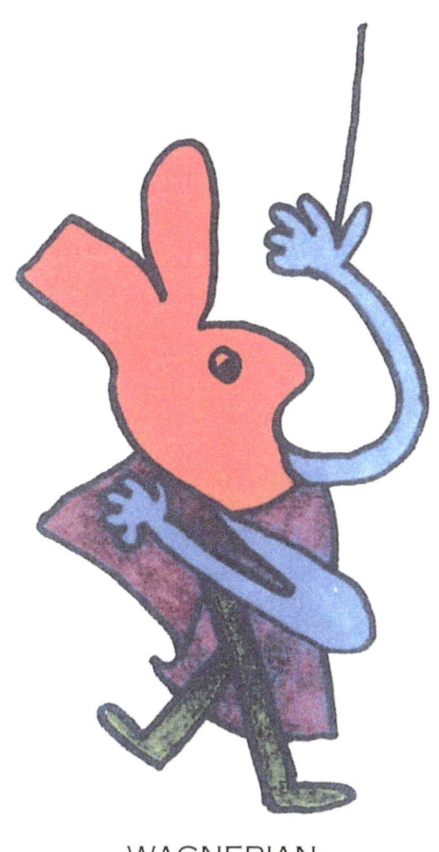

WAGNERIAN

Sometimes I even make strange sounds as I mark the page.

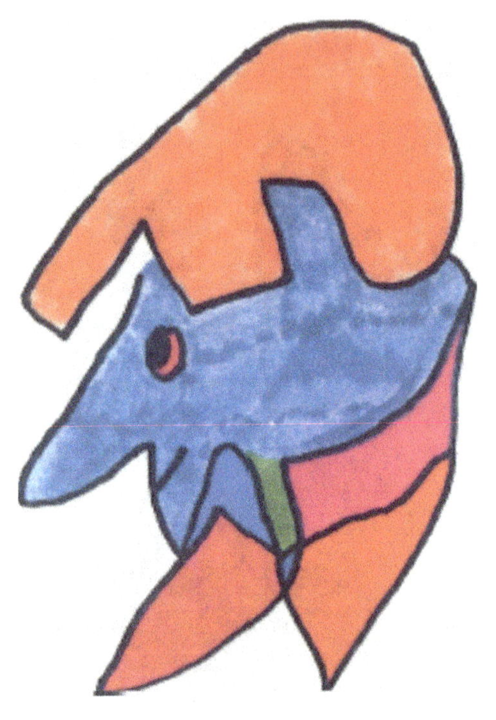

WOLFGANG

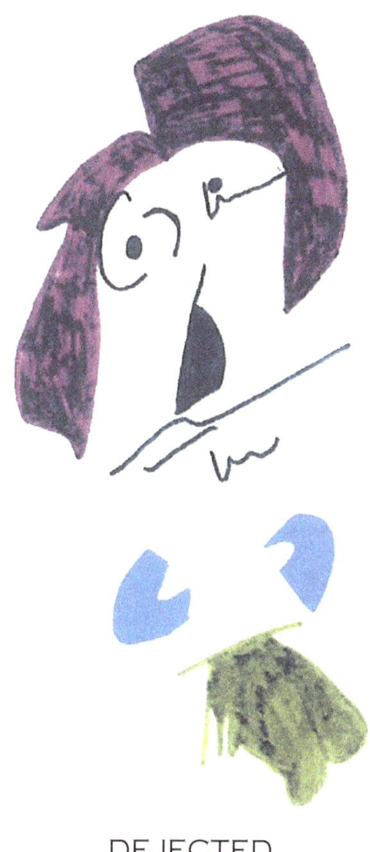

DEJECTED

Occasionally the line breaks apart, the pencil moving in circles or ellipses, sharp points, or in long, flowing lines, or stopping abruptly.

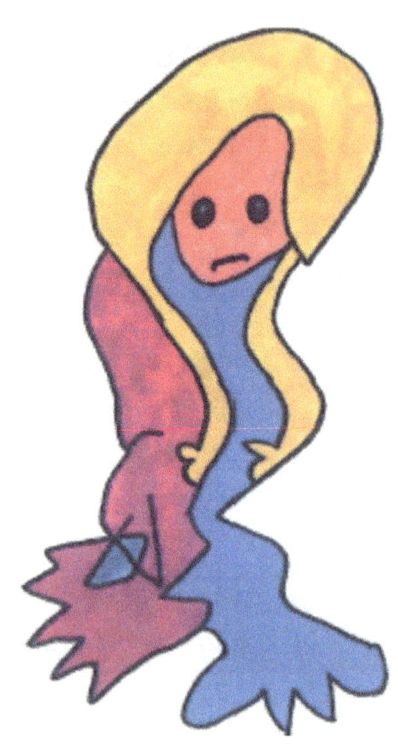

MERMAID

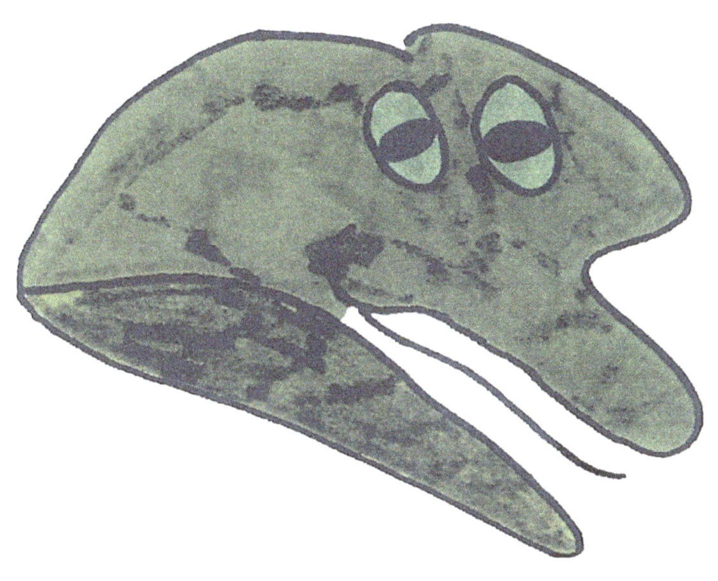

AN OLD FROG

Upon opening my eyes, I can usually recognize a familiar object on the page—

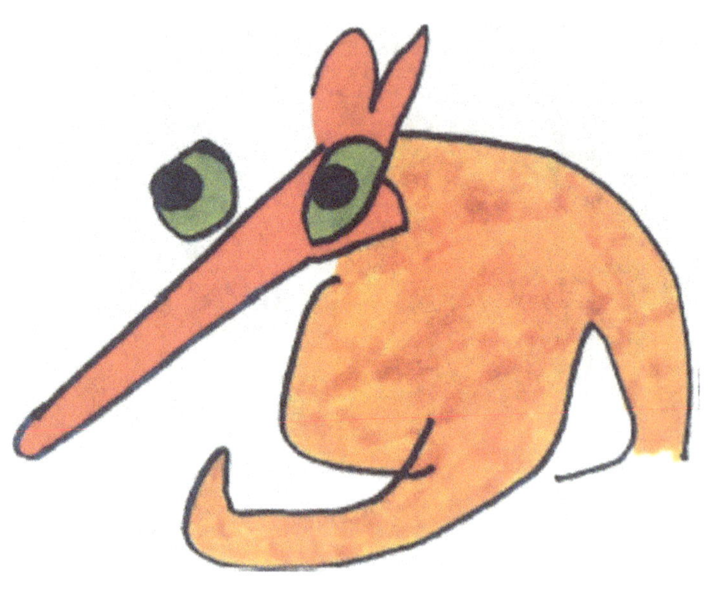

AN ANTEATER, SITTING

as one often sees configurations of all sorts in clouds or
as a sculptor sees an object in a block of uncut stone.

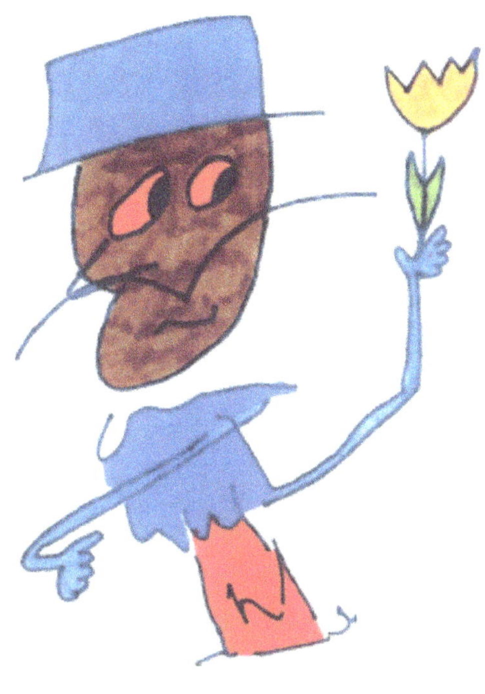

DANDY

If not an animal in a particular pose, I often see a person performing an action or expressing a certain emotional state.

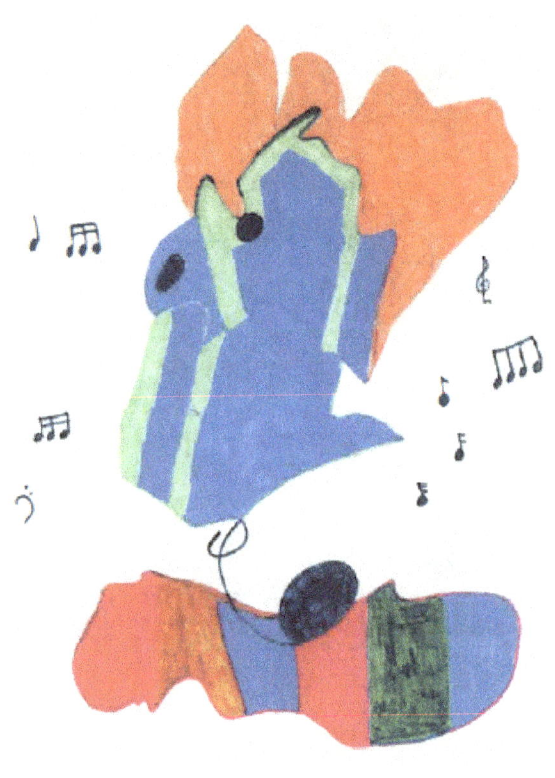

BUST OF BEETHOVEN

Sometimes I see the figures almost madly.

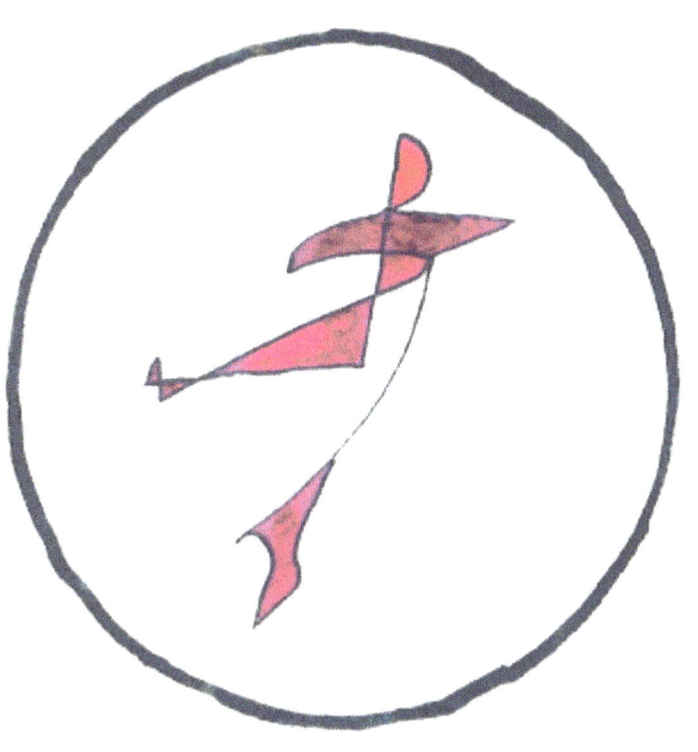

DANCER (IN REDS)

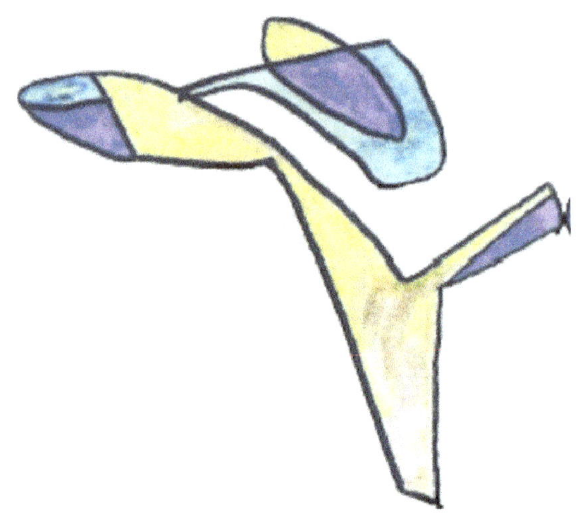

DANCER (IN BLUES)

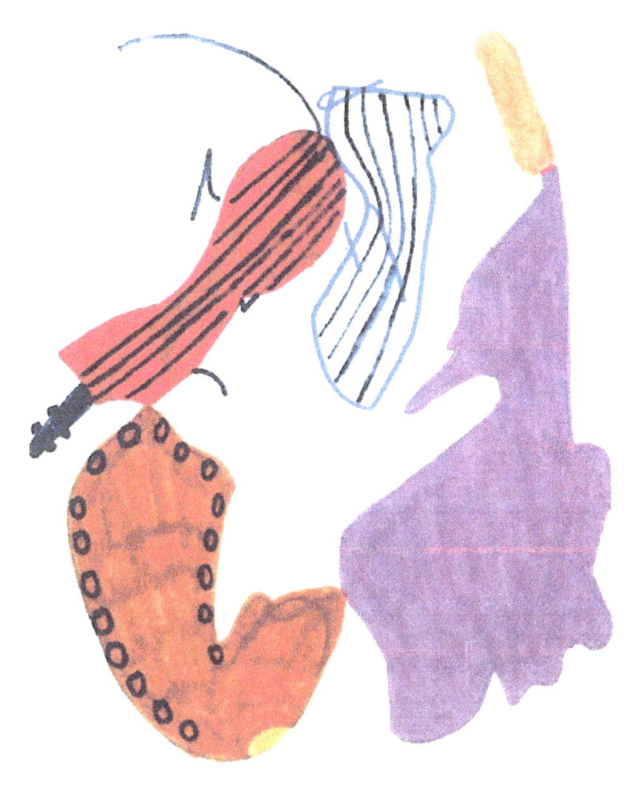

ONE-MAN BAND

Other times, I see it with calm or—

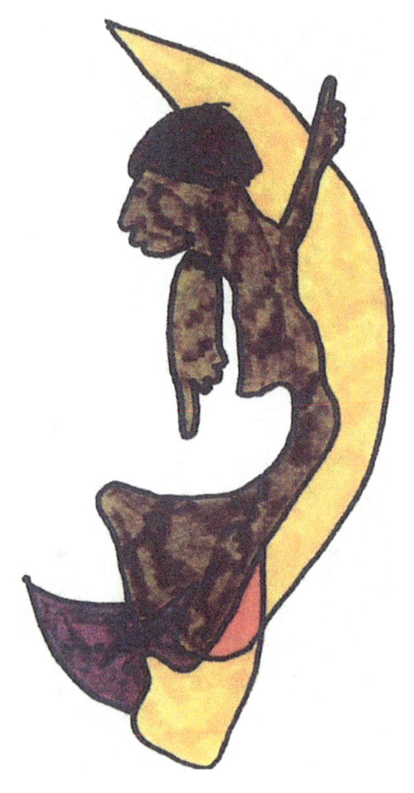

NEANDERTHAL IN THE MOON

in the later seconds of composition—with deliberation.

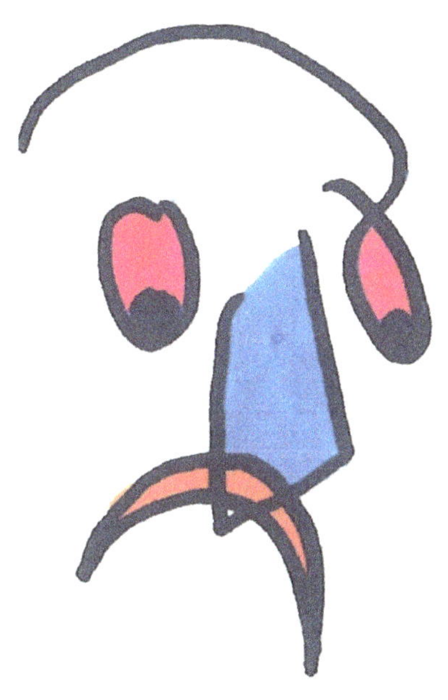

DOWNCAST

Once finished with the initial blind sketch, I sometimes
add an eyelid, lips—

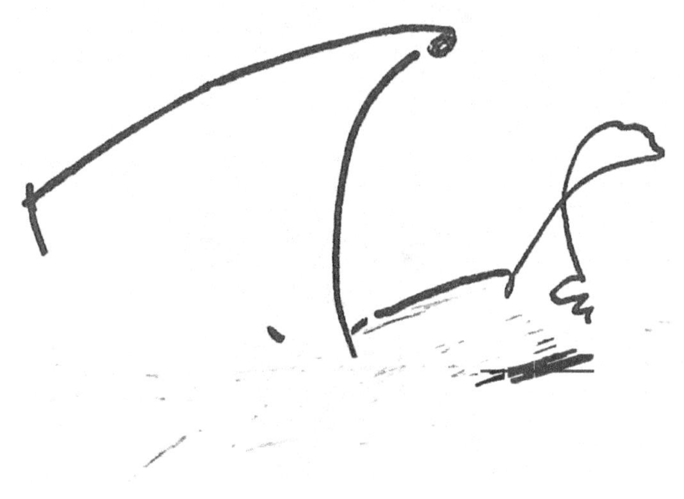

MAN CUTTING BUSH WITH SCYTHE

or even so tiny a mark as a dot (which, ironically, can alter the entire "presence" of the picture).

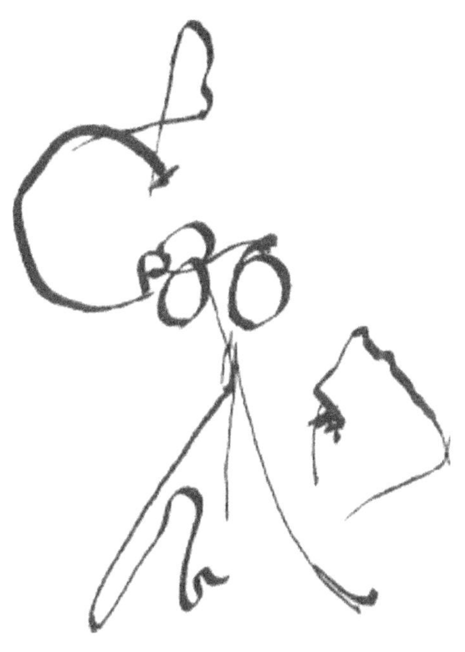

CYMBALIST

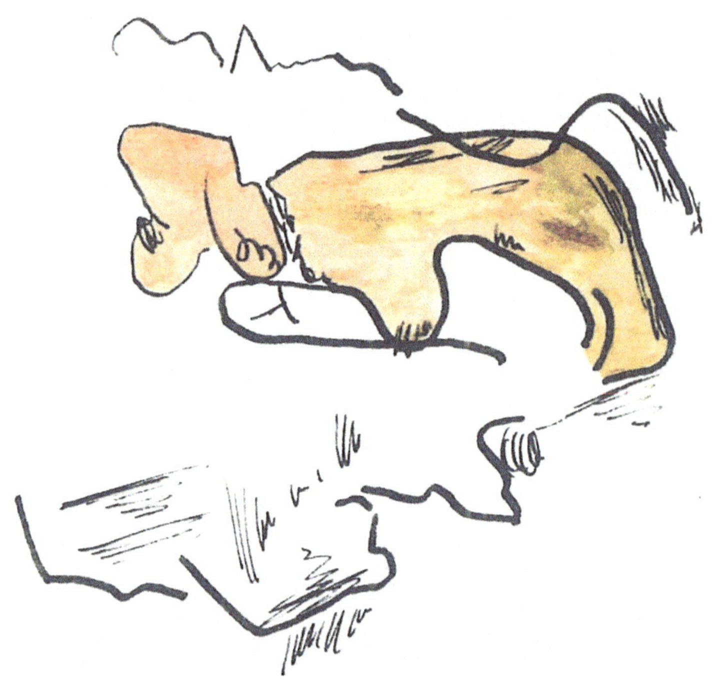

DOG OVERLOOKING CLIFF

Whatever emerges from the scribbles as interesting becomes the picture as defined by the imagination.

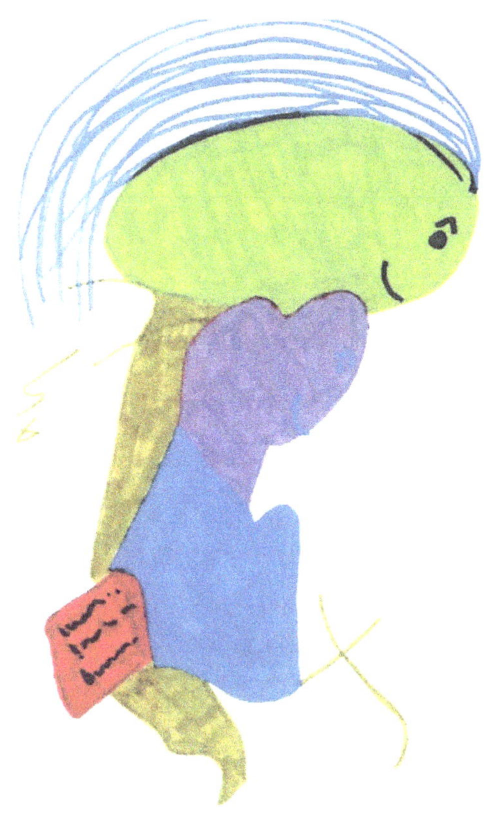

MOTHER AND CHILD WITH BOOK

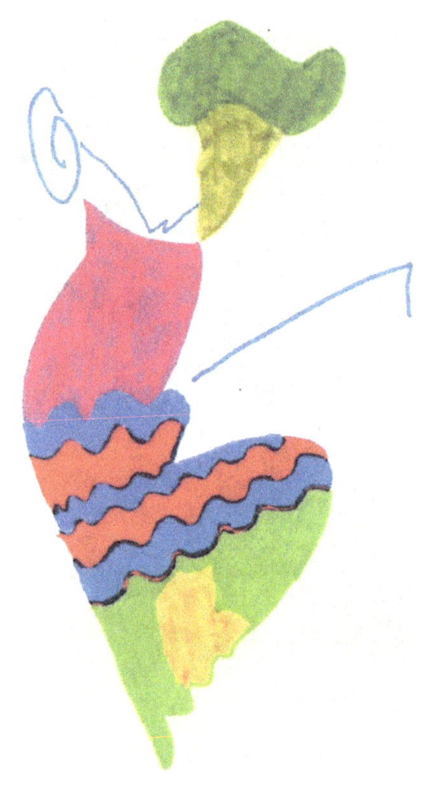

FLAMENCO DANCER

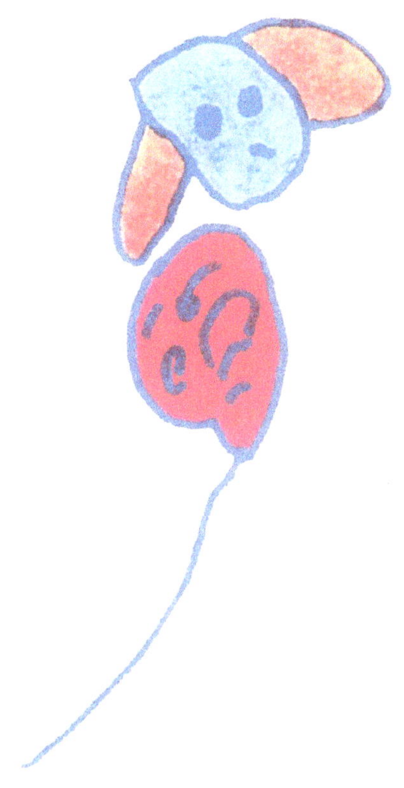

A TAIL WELL TOLD

Sometimes the title comes early, at other times in the
last stages of composition —

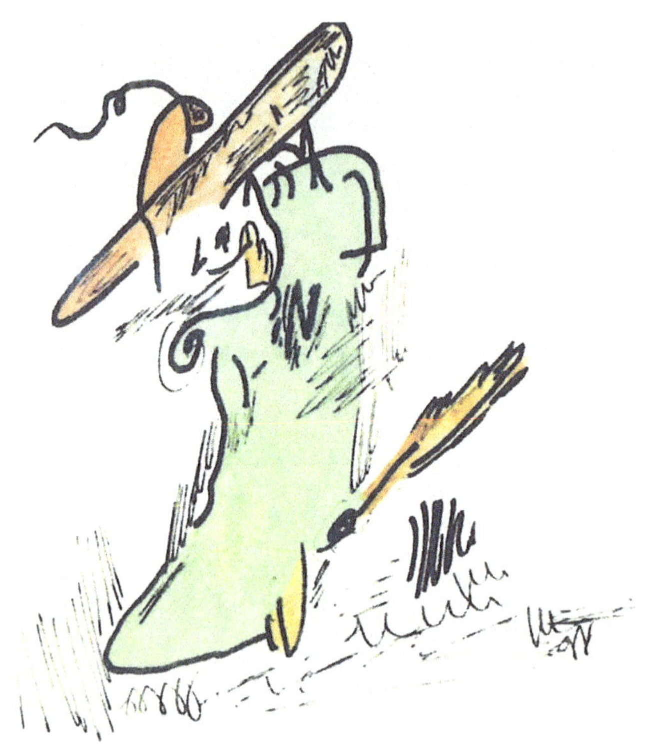

GIGGLING SPANIARD

during which I sometimes add a dot here, a tiny flourish there, a ball or a small flower or strokes at the edges of a mouth—infinitesimal changes but as significant in the creation of meaning as punctuation in a poem.

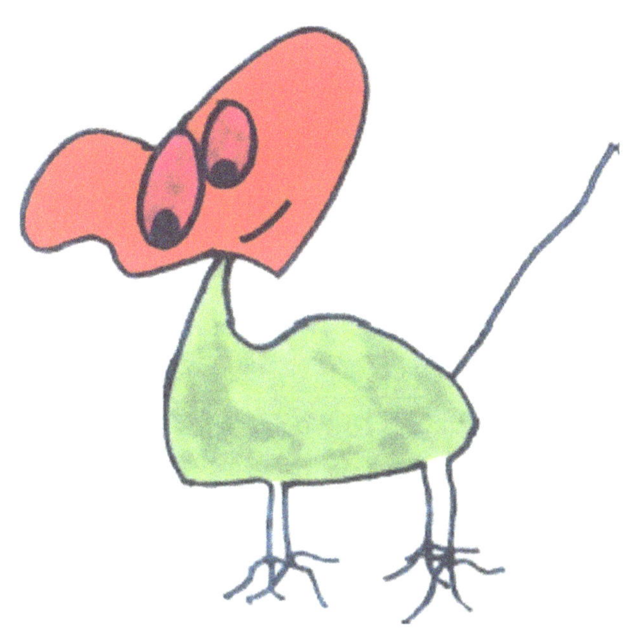

BIG HEARTED

Once the picture seems finished, I refrain from altering
any of its compositional parts.

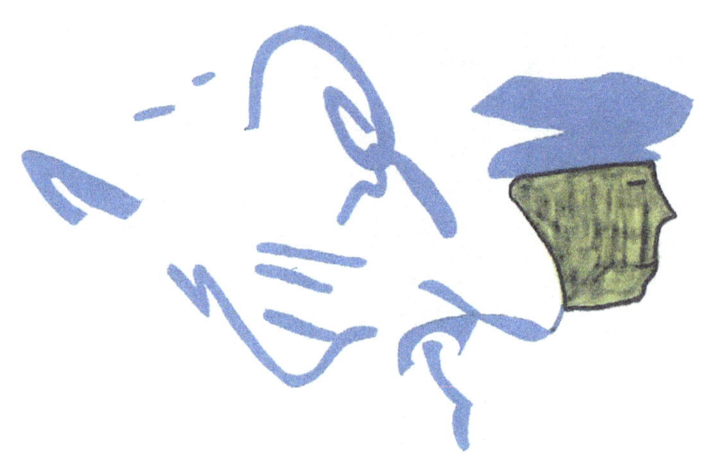

HOW THE SELF SHREDS

Because I am both poet and sculptor, I think I can best explain or describe blind drawing in terms of those quite distinct experiences of creation.

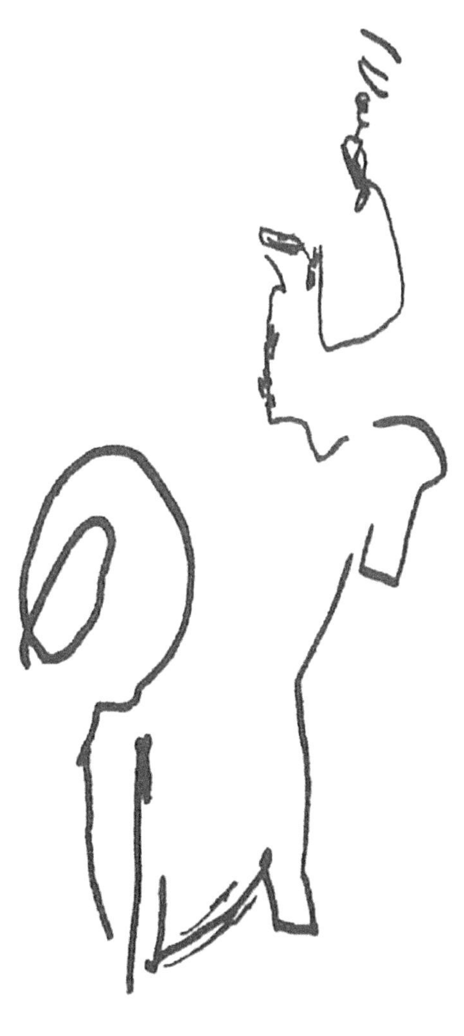

ERECT MOOSE

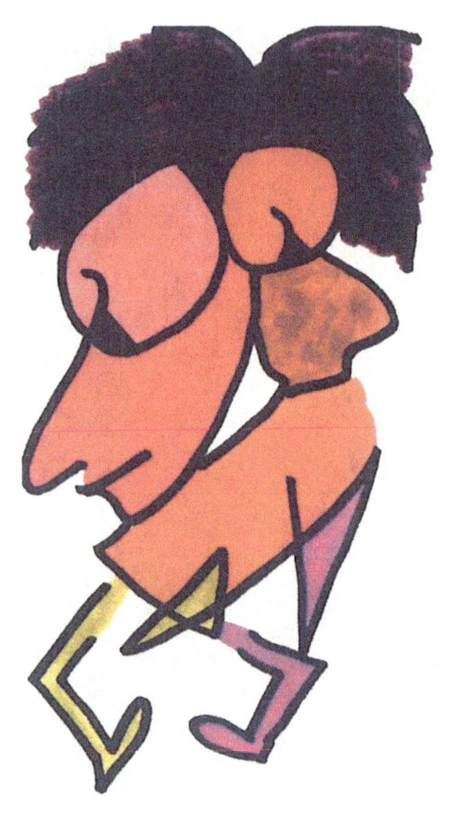

SPLIT PERSONALITY

Both poetry and sculpture demand far longer periods of creative exercise.

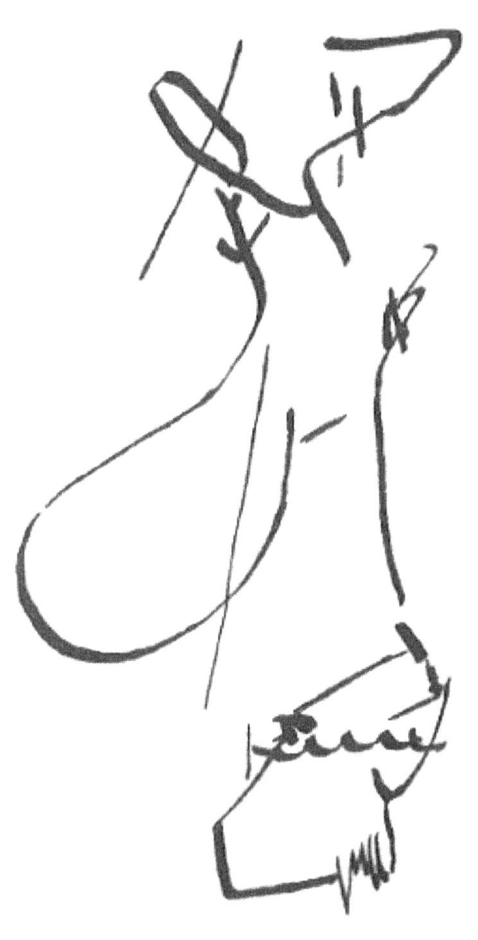

MOOSE WITH CAKE

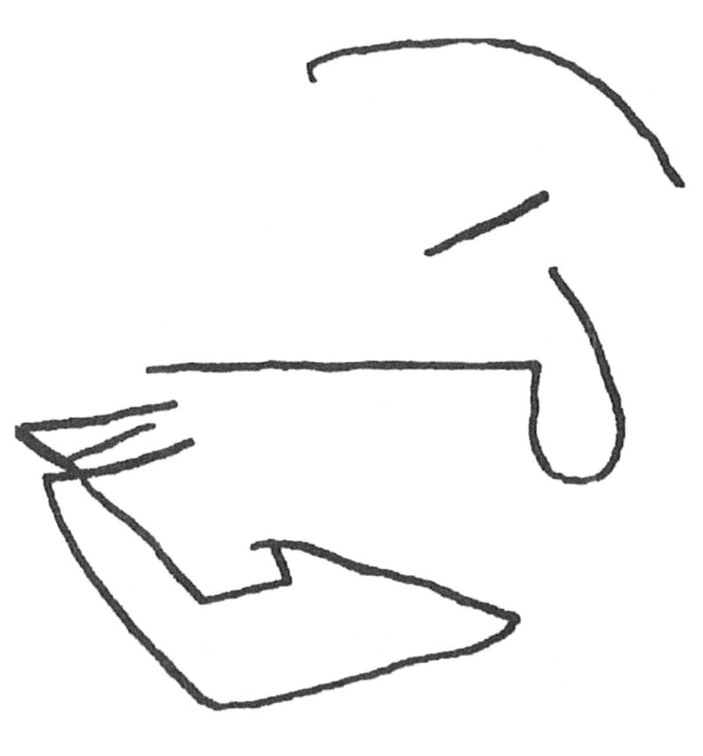

MAN LOOKING AT PALM

Because these drawings depend upon an immediacy
and brief intensity,

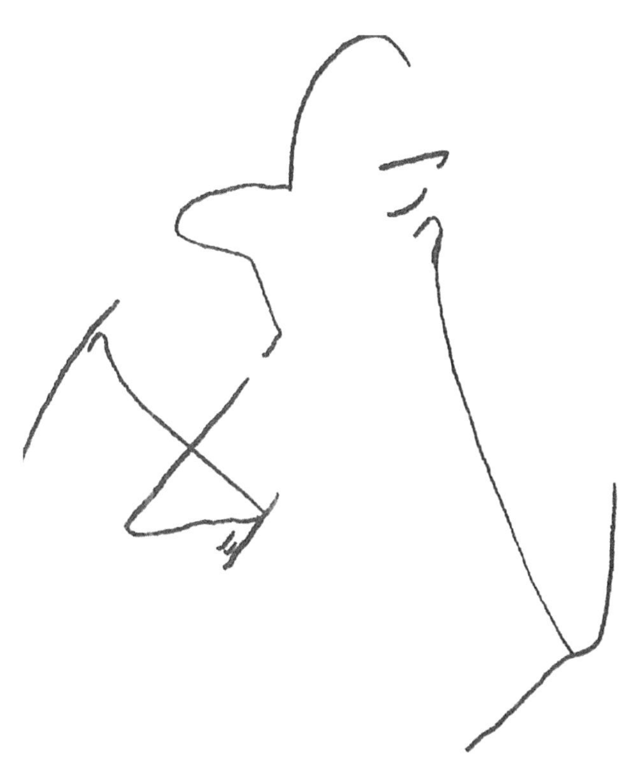

MAN WITH A STICK

the   experience,   for   me,   is   not   unlike   suddenly
conceiving the idea for a poem.

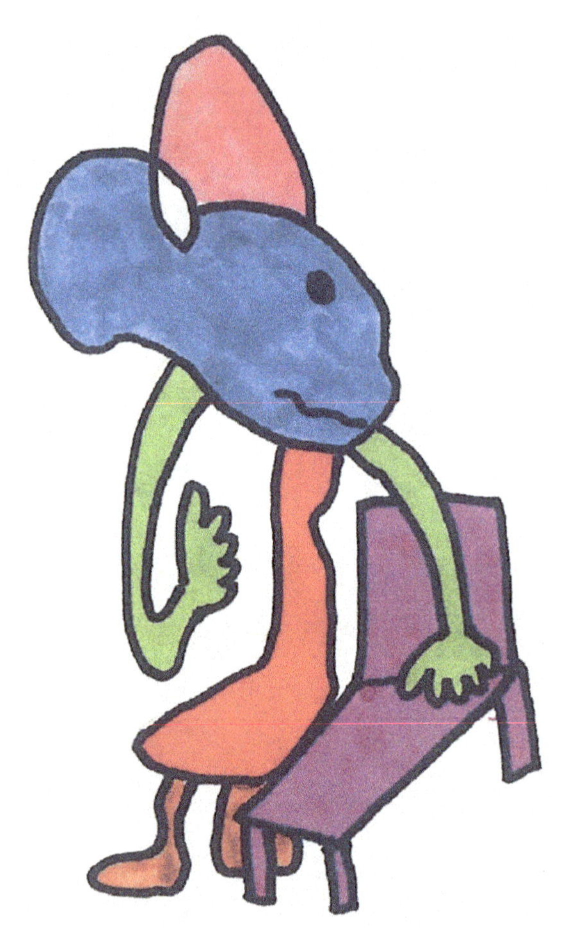

PREPARING TO SIT

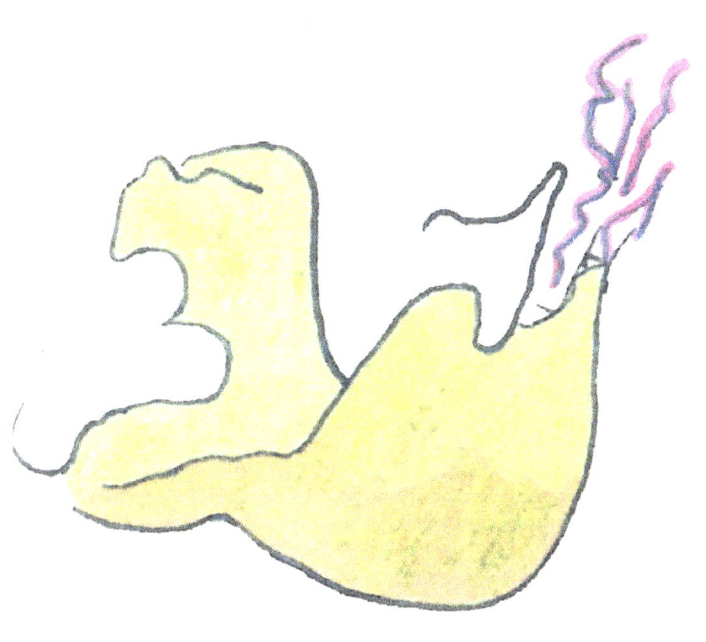

TURTLE ON FIRE

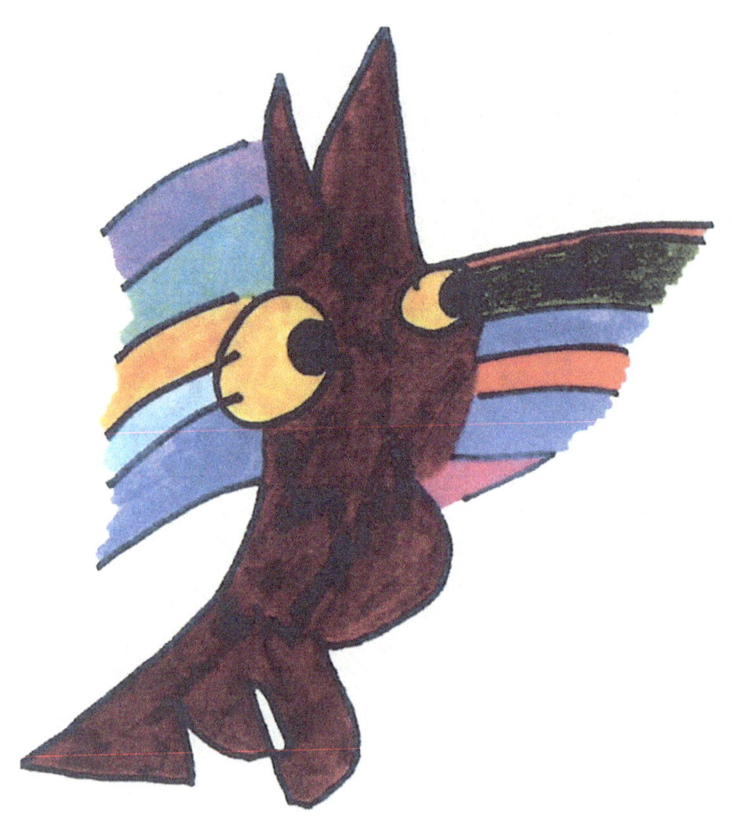

RAINBOW

The outburst of vision that becomes a drawing is then followed by the more "decorative" work—

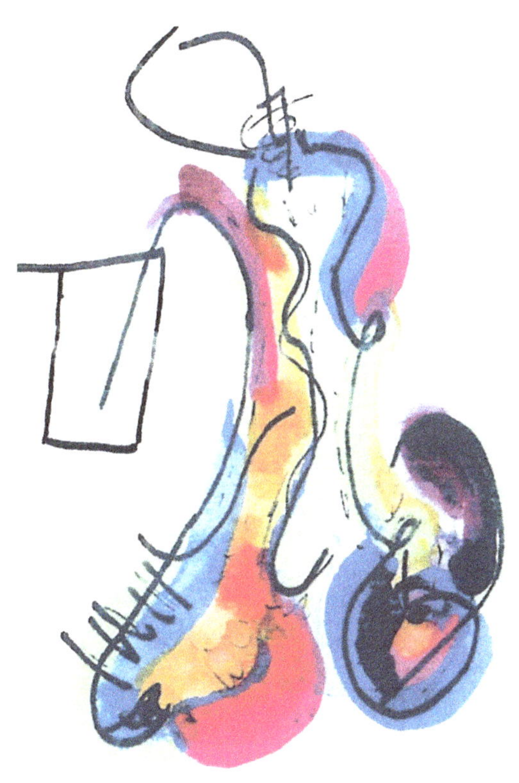

DRESSED TO KILL

not unlike the feverish first draft of a poem, which is
then edited, elaborated, formalized, polished.

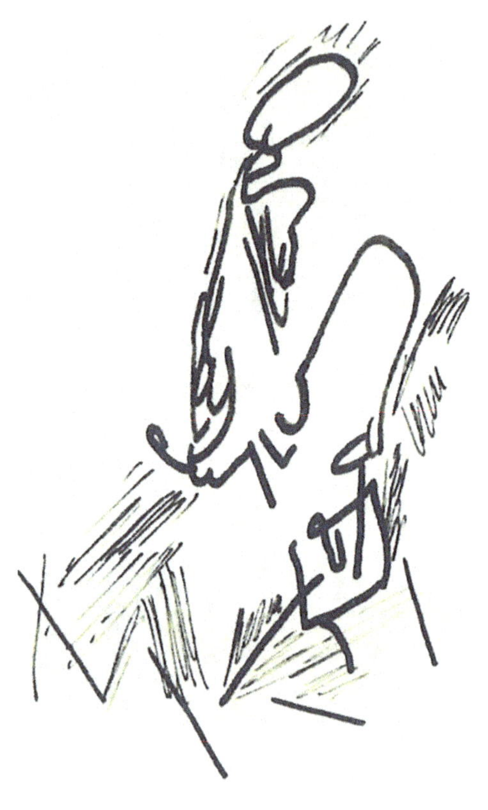

GIRL BY CANDLE

But I think it fair to say that the drawings are more like
sculpture than poetry—

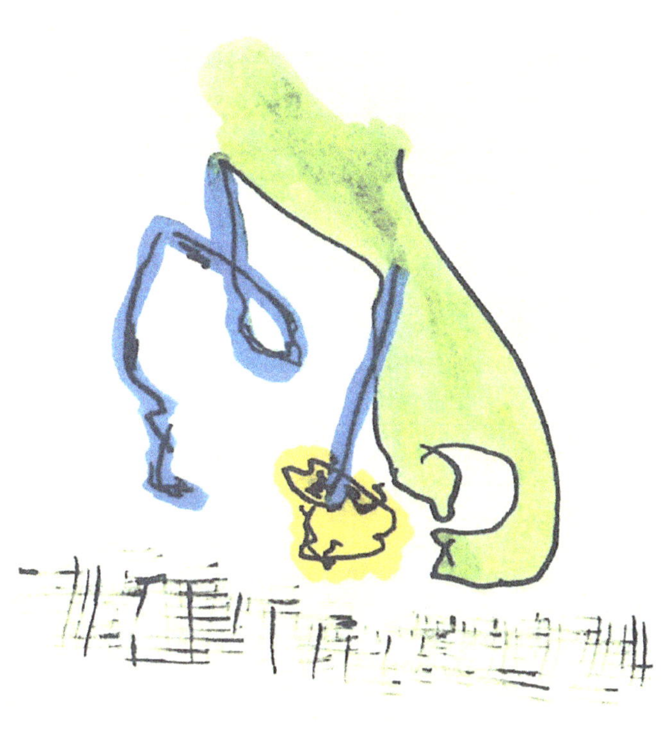

WAXING THE KITCHEN FLOOR

since they are composed of things without definitions (shapes), not like words but more like body lines.

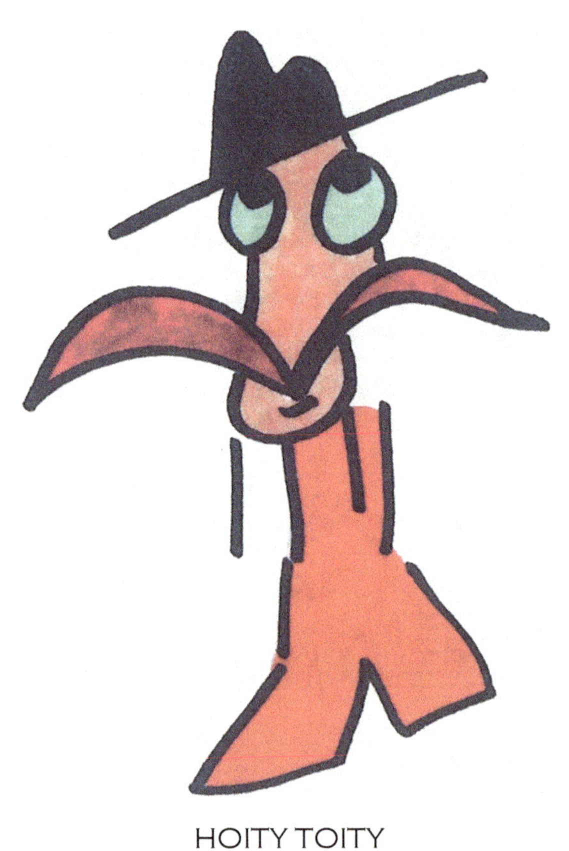

HOITY TOITY

As with sculpture, the drawings contain an aspect of "discovery," a seeing something in a raw or unworked piece.

56

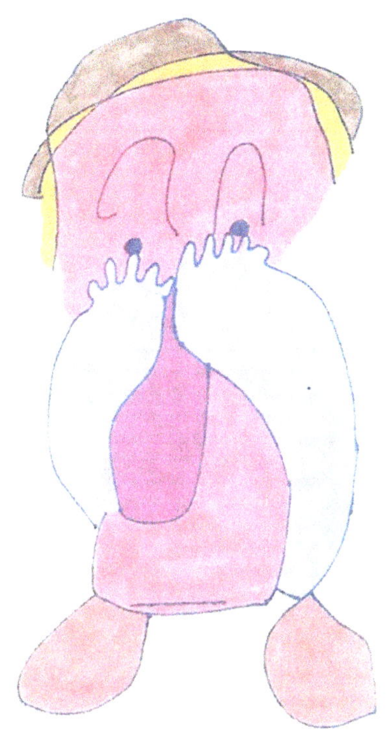

EMBARRASSED

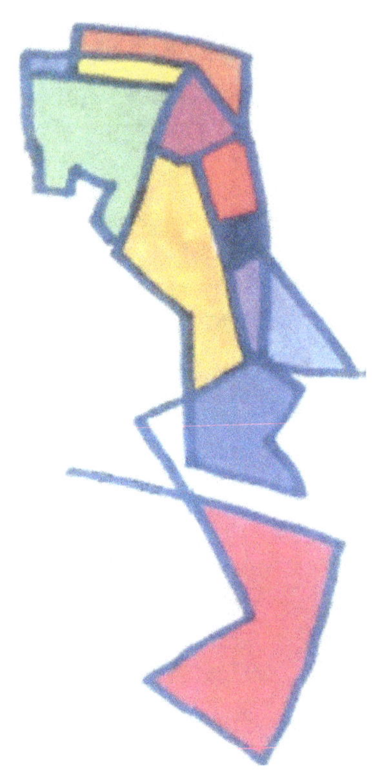

STAINED GLASS MAN

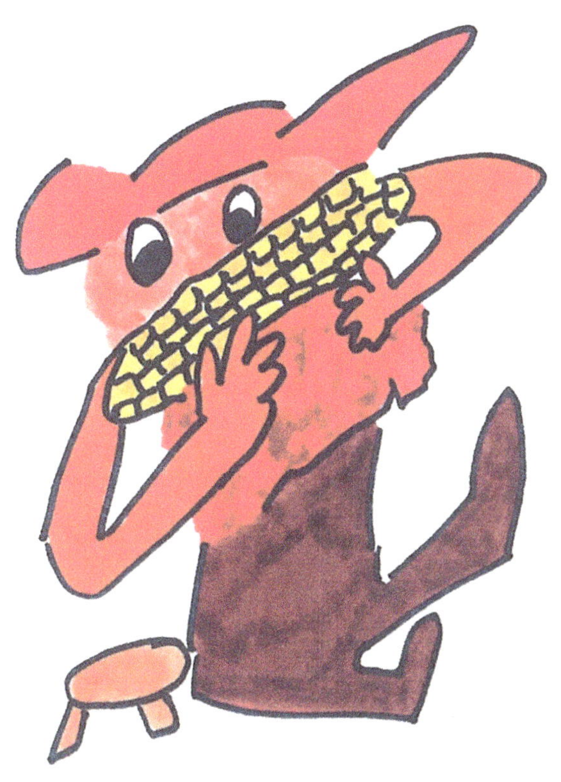

EATING CORN

As the sculptor sees a figure in a block of clay, I see in the scribbles on the page a person who is chewing, a dog baying, a dancer, a fisherman, and so forth.

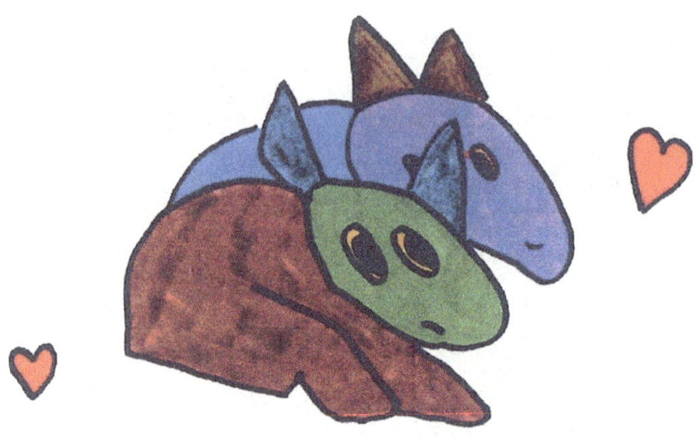

IN LOVE

In poetry, however, the process of discovery on the part
of the artist lasts a lot longer—

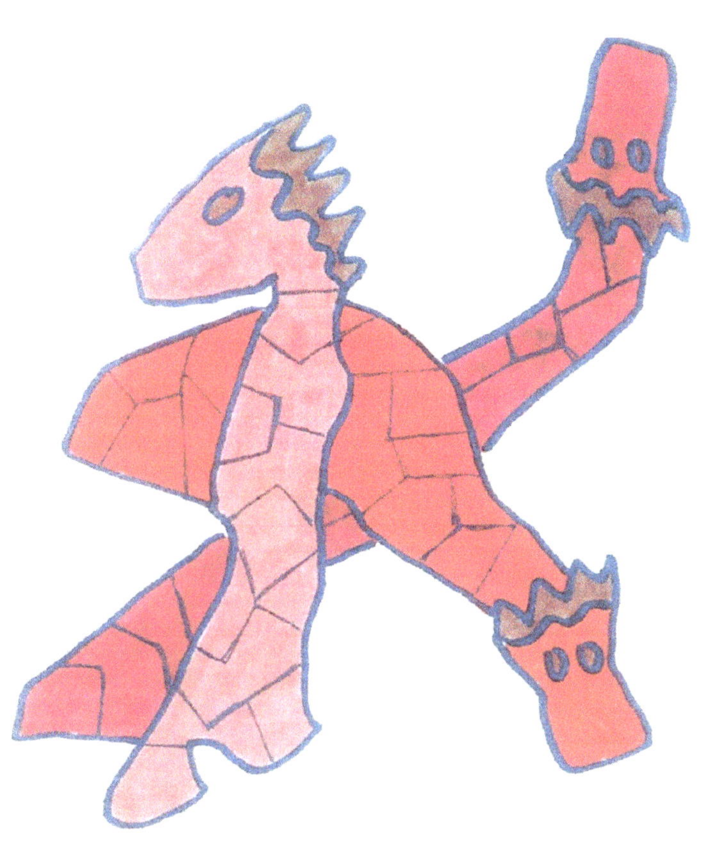

LOVE TRIANGLE

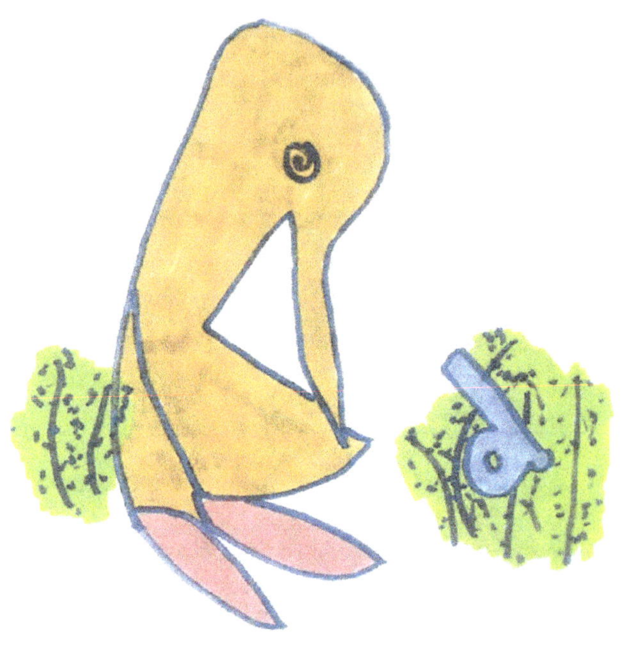

SITTING DUCK

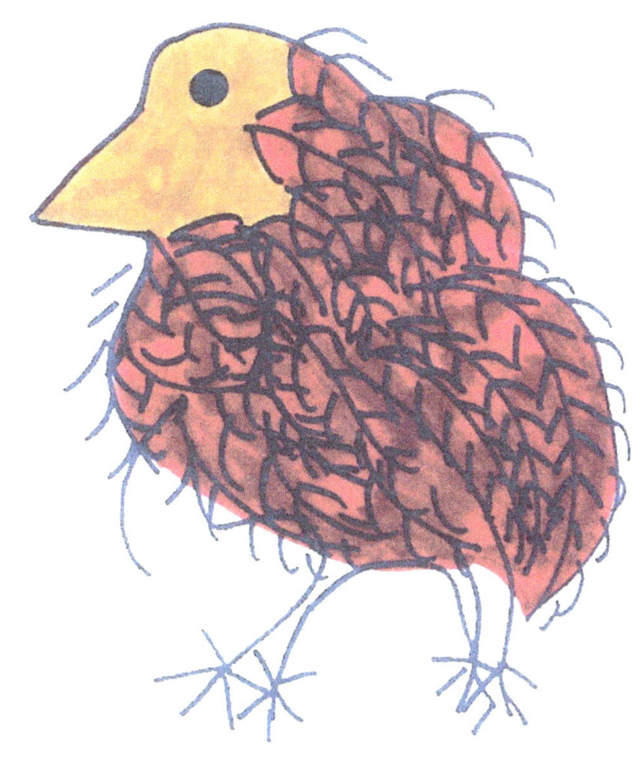

UNRUFFLED

since the poet does not actually "see" in the words a
picture or a form and does not really mold the words
into a concrete shape.

PIANIST

Nor does the poet see personalities in apparently random markings on a blank page.

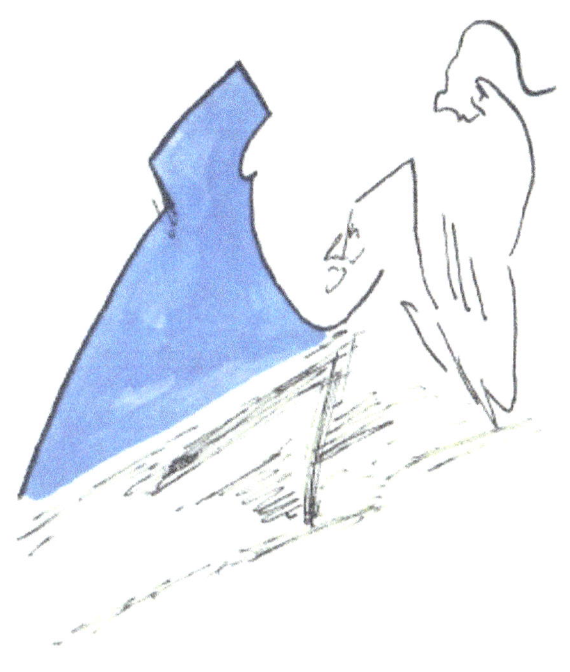

HOROWITZ

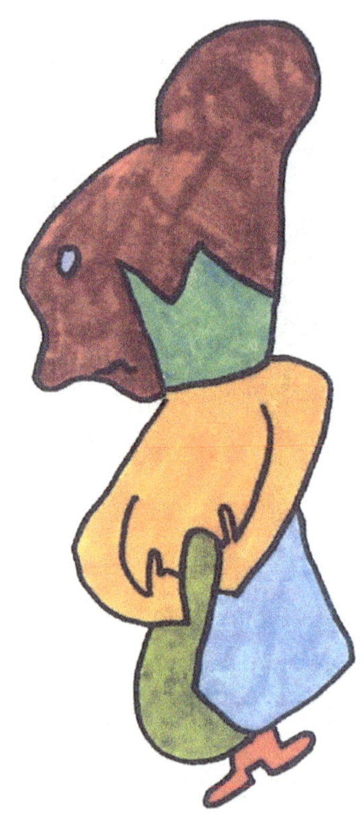

GRANDMOTHER, HIGH COLLARED

for the drawings can easily be passed around and communicated and shared with many people at once through the distribution of my notebooks of drawings and through the publication of this book.

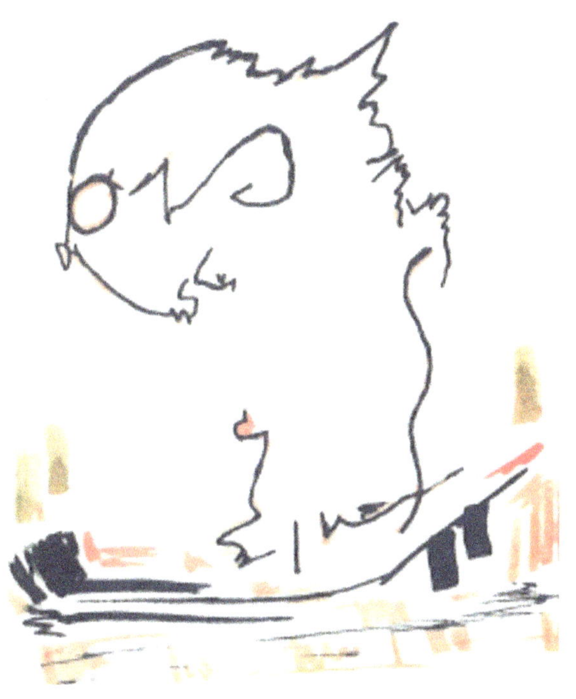

OWL

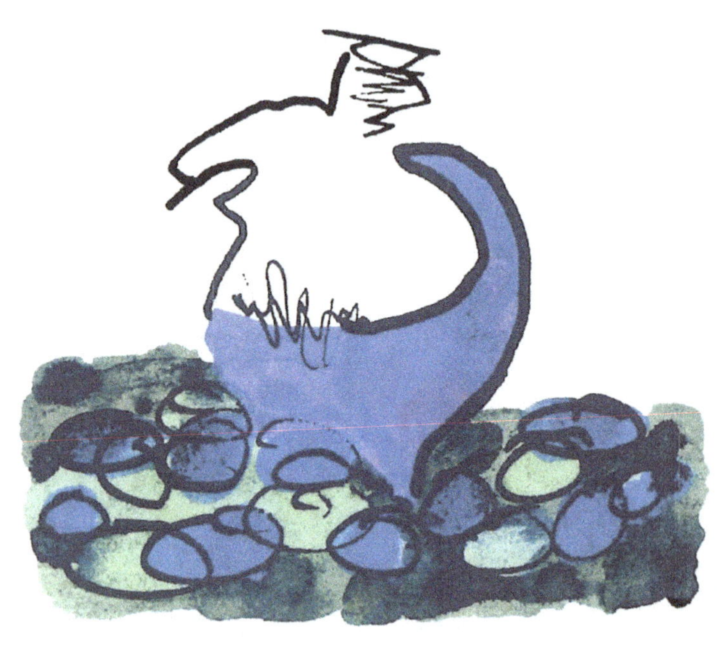

MAN FIGHTING WAVES

I think the drawings constitute more or less a passage through the many affective states of an individual being in the world.

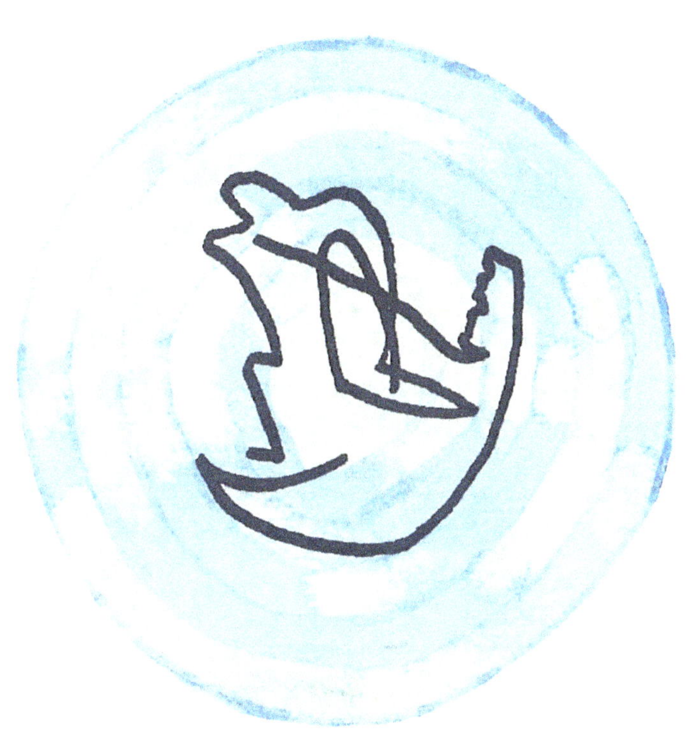

ROWING

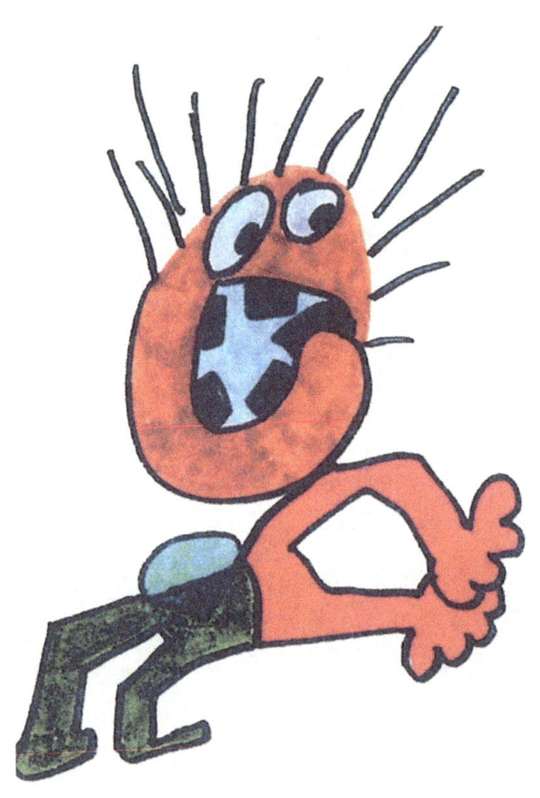

RAGE

Some of the drawings are comic and some sad,

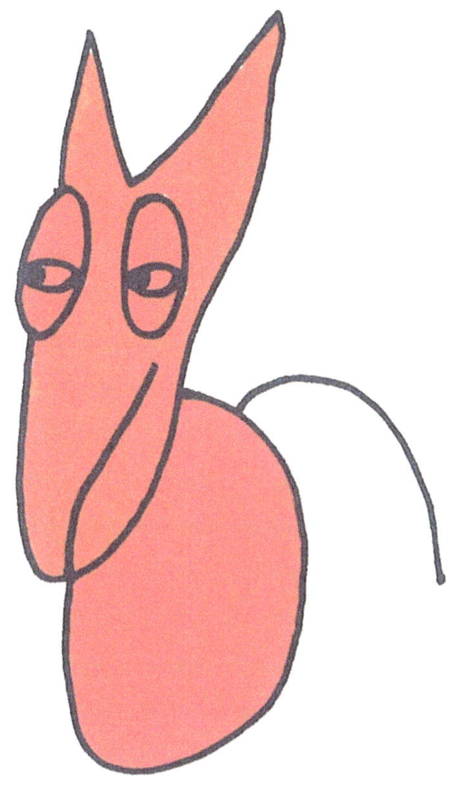

FOXY

but with a kind of tangible guile.

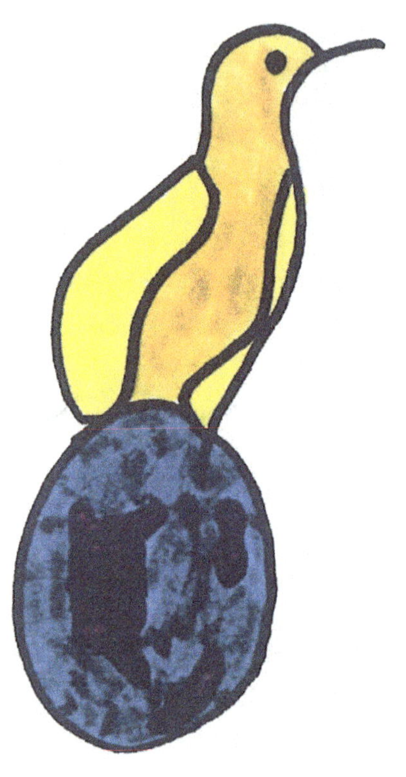

PERSPECTIVE

I would hope that the discovery for the audience would
be delight at seeing something new—

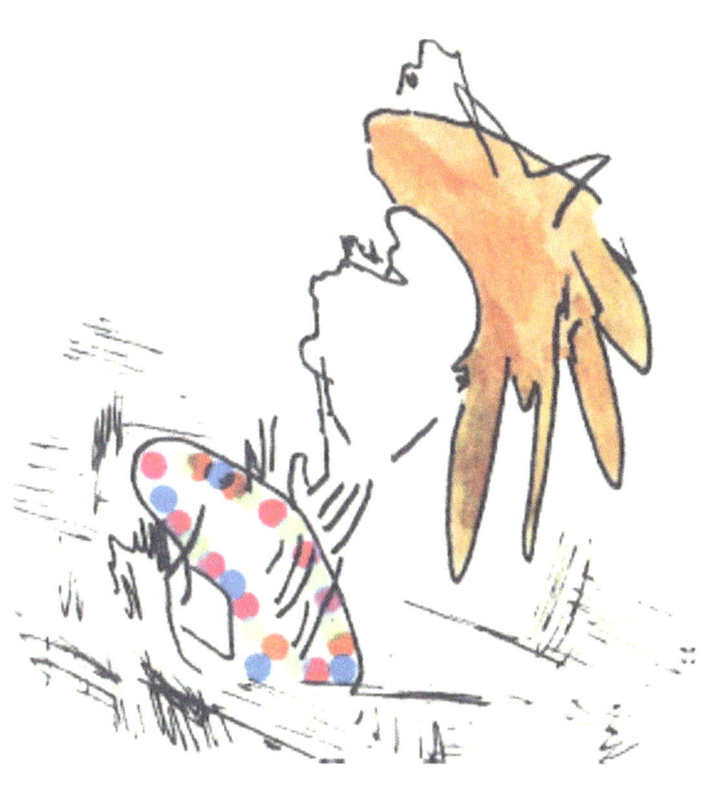

INDIAN WITH EASEL

something unexpected, beyond anticipation.

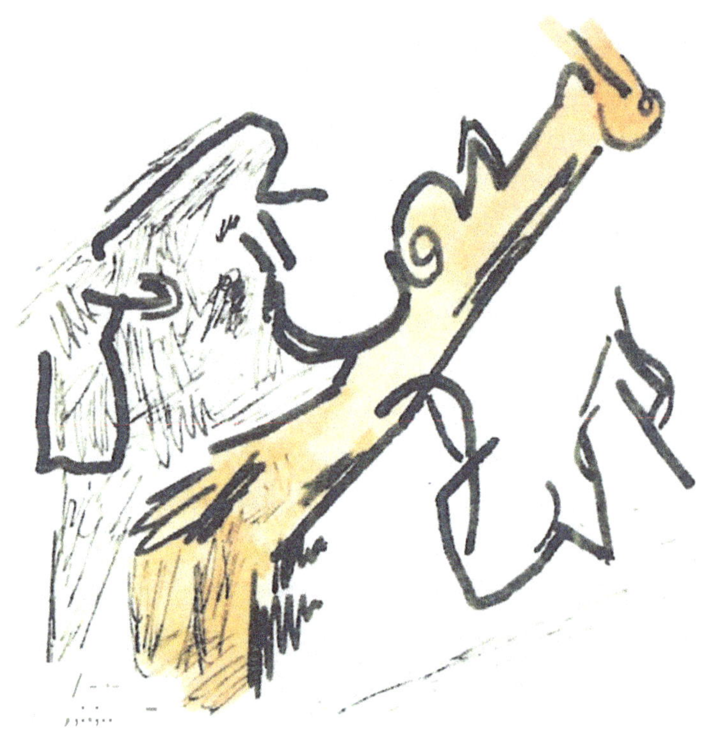

BASSOONIST

I would hope that the process of discovery in the viewer
of these drawings would mirror that of the artist—

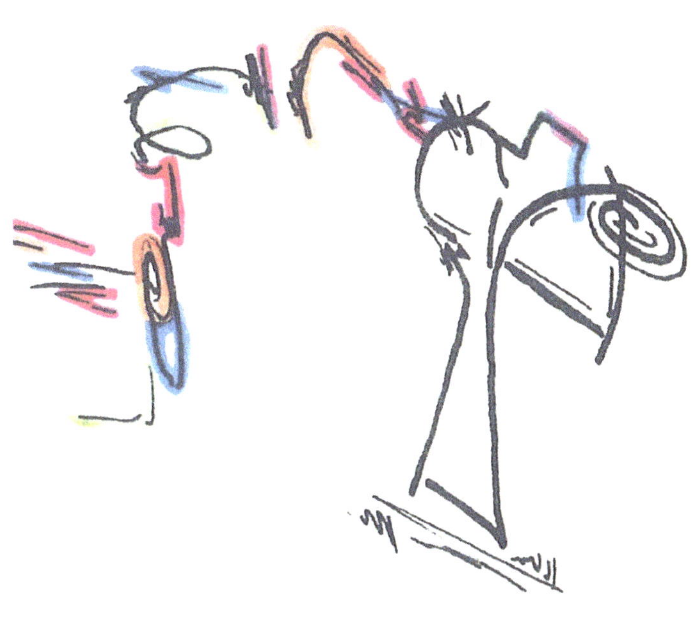

HARMONICS OF A YOUNG VIOLINIST

that the viewer, although seeing the title of the drawing, would take at least a minute or two until saying, "Yes, yes, that's what it is . . . I see it now."

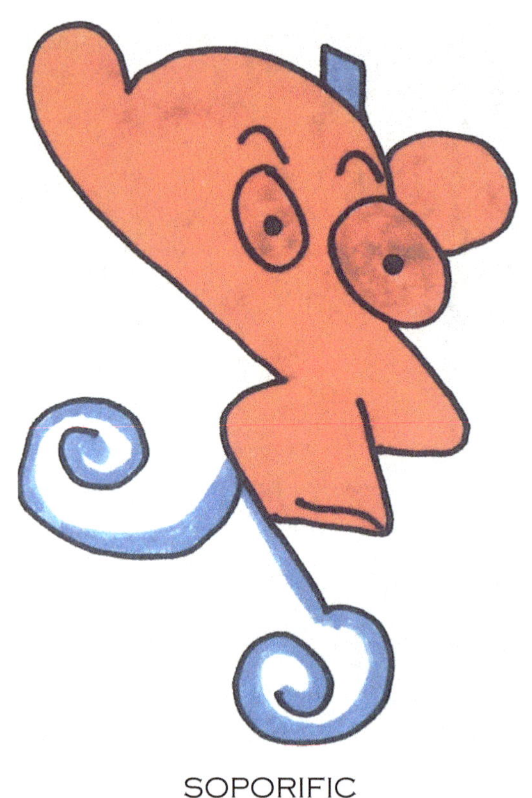

SOPORIFIC

My mother once recalled to me her thrill at discovering the meaning of a phrase in Pope's *Dunciad*. She said she often experiences that kind of thrill of "seeing" while reading poetry.

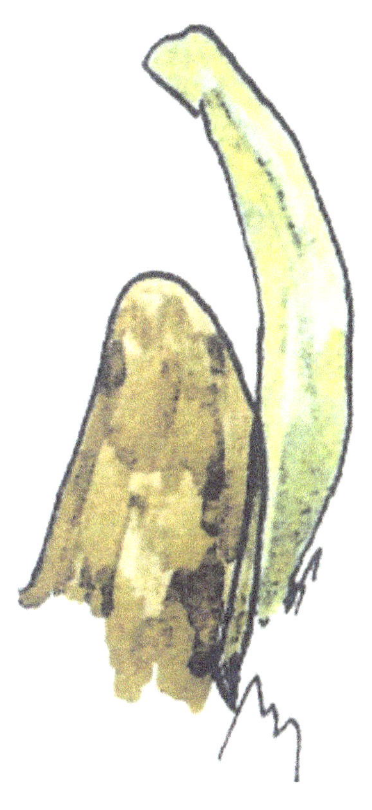

MONK ON ROCK

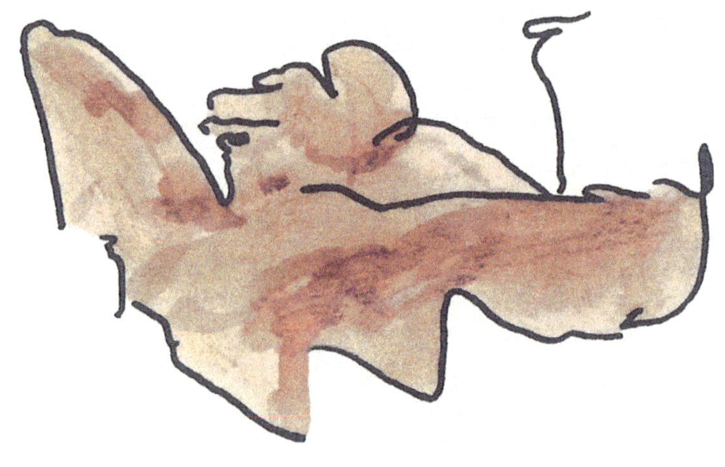

SMOKING PELICAN

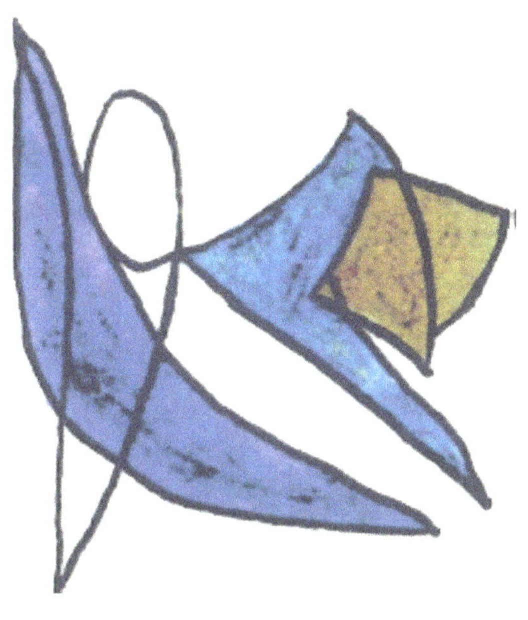

WOMAN WAVING TWO SCARVES

I would love to think that when you first look at one of my blind drawings, your experience would be somewhat similar, that you will suddenly feel that thrill.

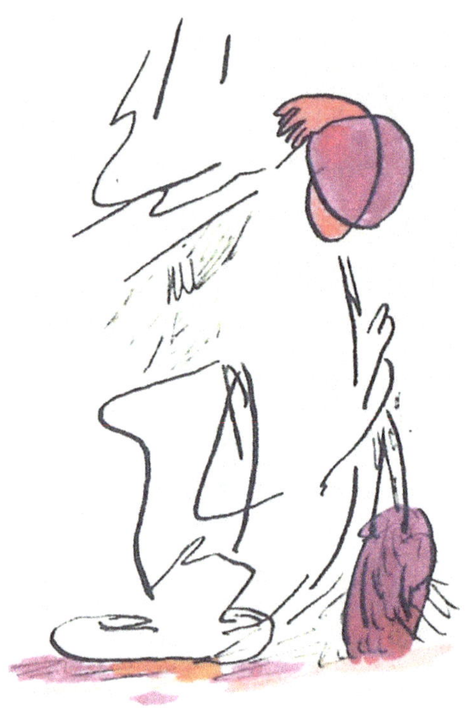

HOUSEWIFE WITH MOP

My drawings are small things, neither profound nor distilling of human greatness.

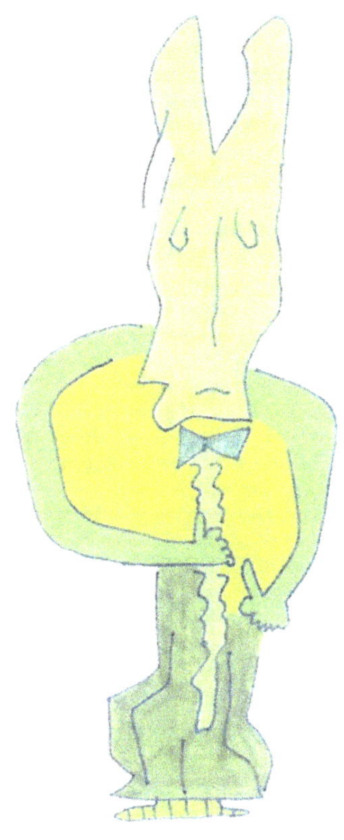

FORMAL

Nevertheless, you might look at one of them as you might a piece of abstract sculpture you've never seen before.

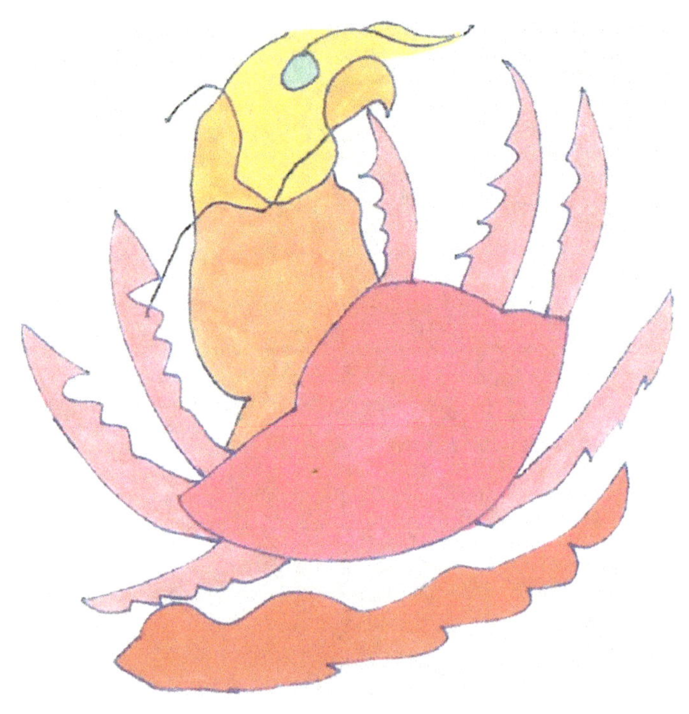

BIRD ON SOFT-SHELL CRAB

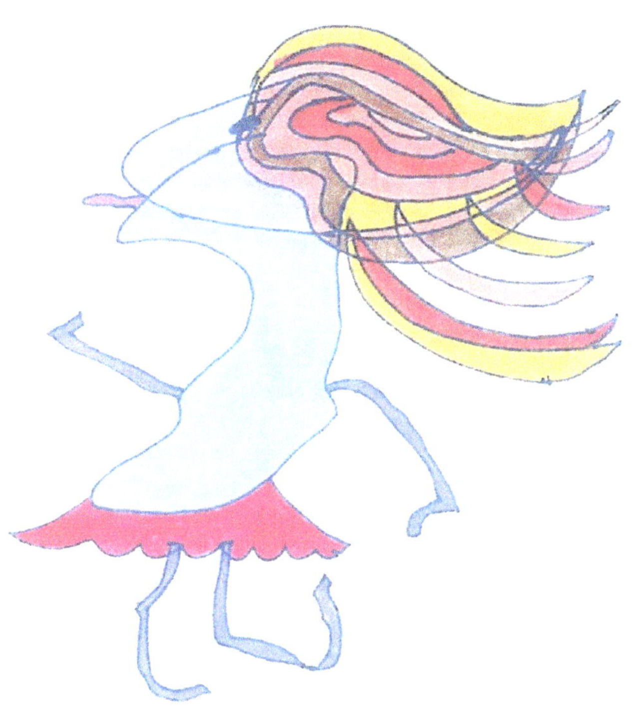

MISBEHAVIOR

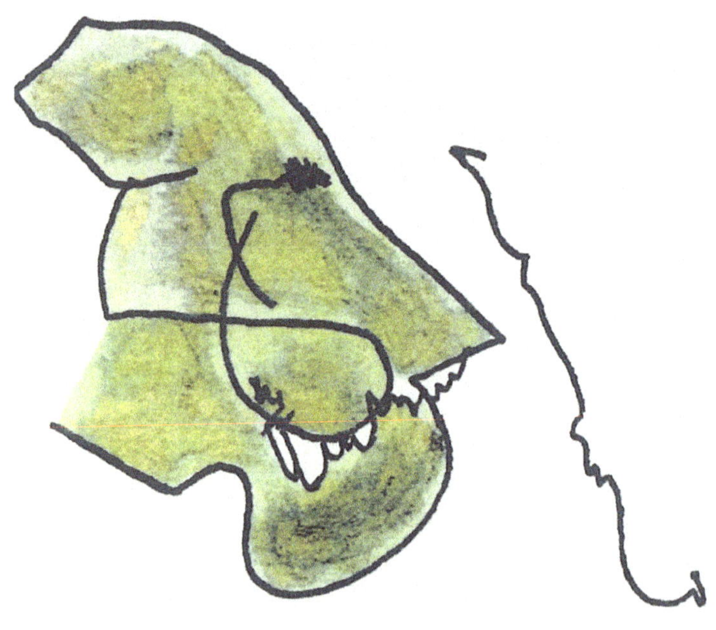

SKULL

Viewers of abstract sculpture often experience a
"discovery," a seeing of something in shape and texture
and flow of line, just as the sculptor himself has seen it
in a block of clay or wood or stone,

84

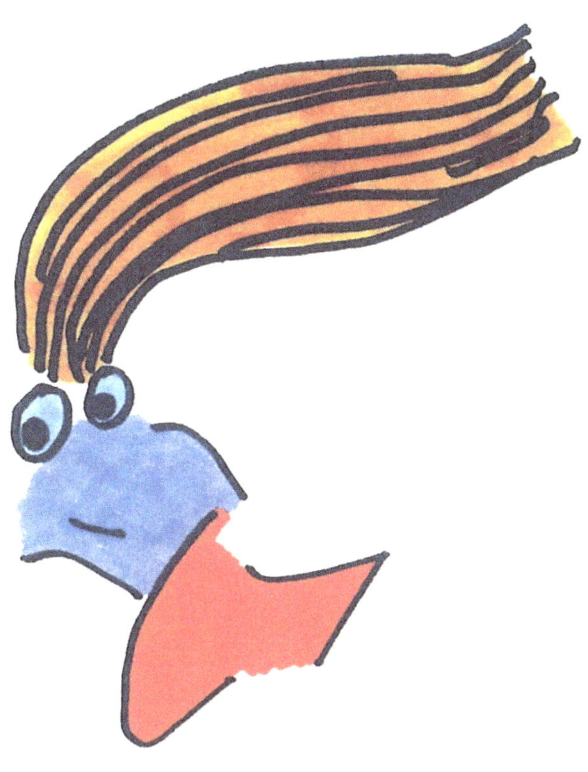

WINDSWEPT

as a child sees in the shape of a cloud a person or a
monster or something entirely beautiful.

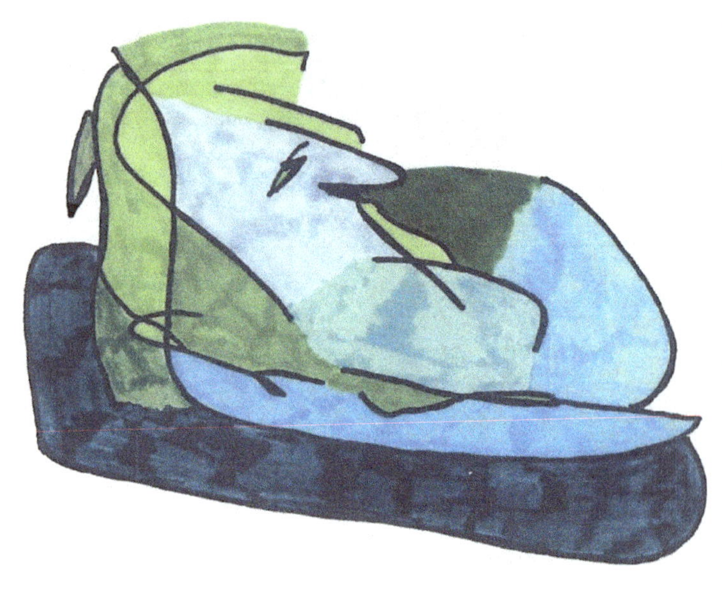

PSYCHOANALYSIS

I mean only to say that each of these drawings represents the mirror images of an experience shared by creator and audience.

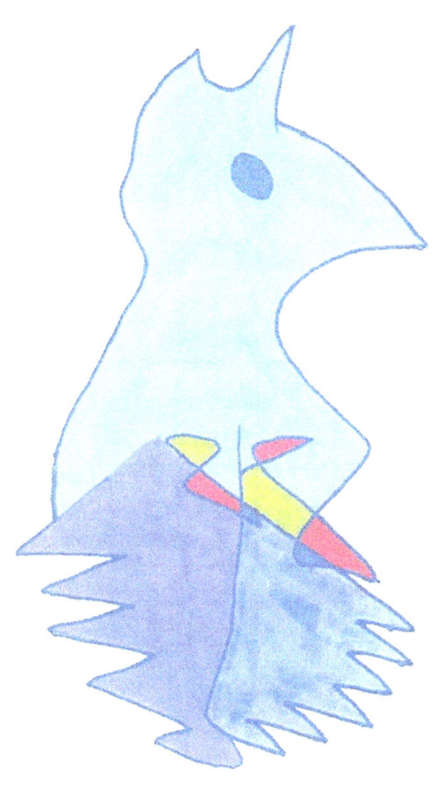

QUIETUDE

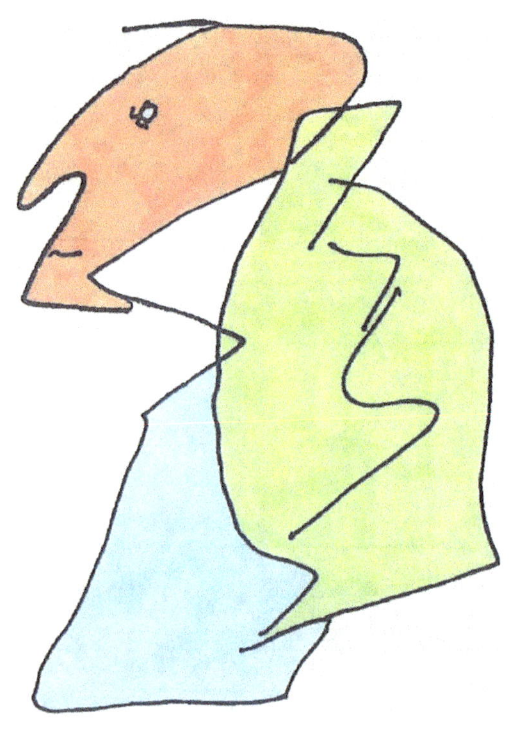

OSTEOPOROSIS

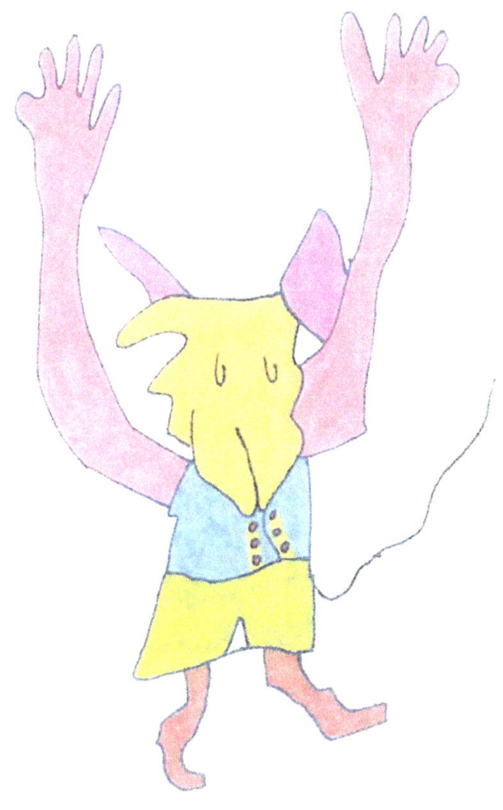

Many of these drawings are comic, even jokes, making
fun of our happy and often poignant foolishness.

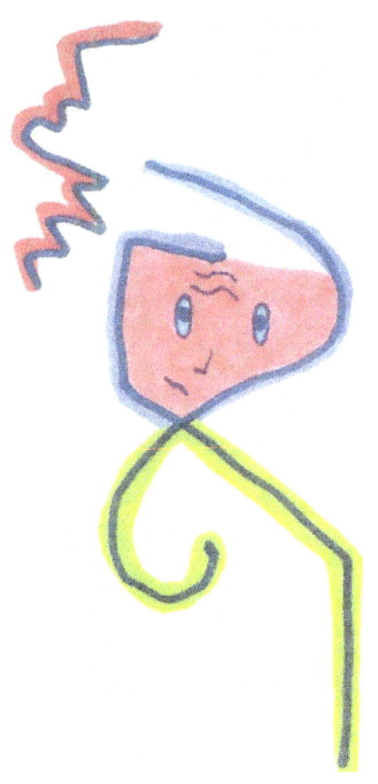

TRAUMA

Some are sad, but with a duplicity that draws on how we, at our best, handle sorrow.

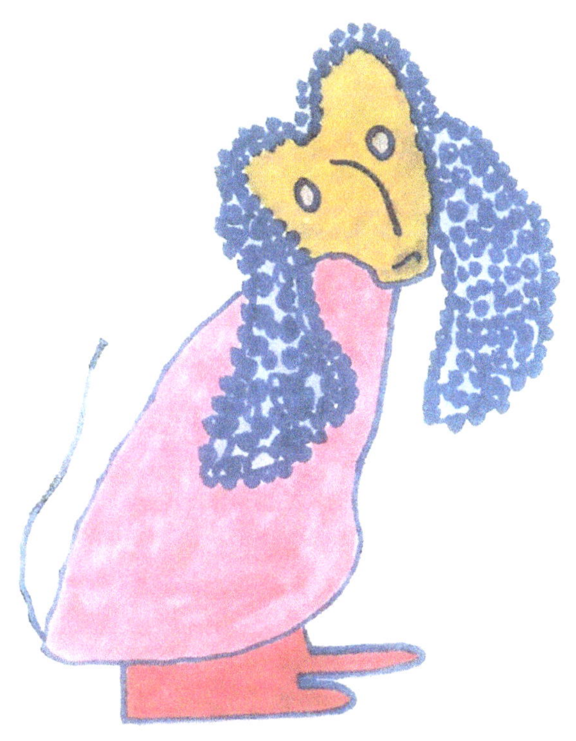

RENAISSANCE HOUND

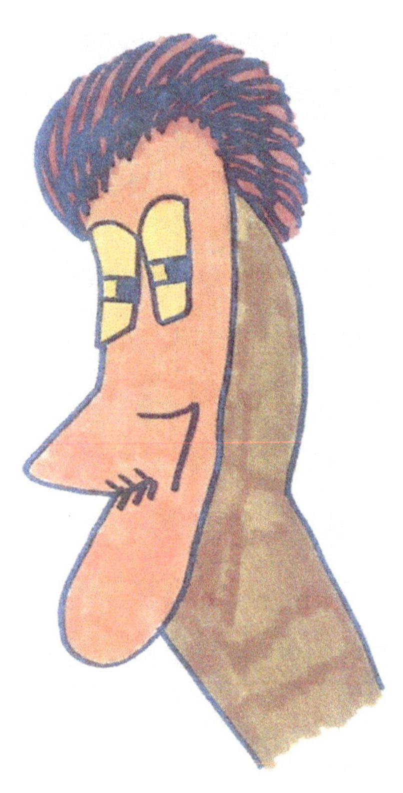

AFTER DENTAL SURGERY

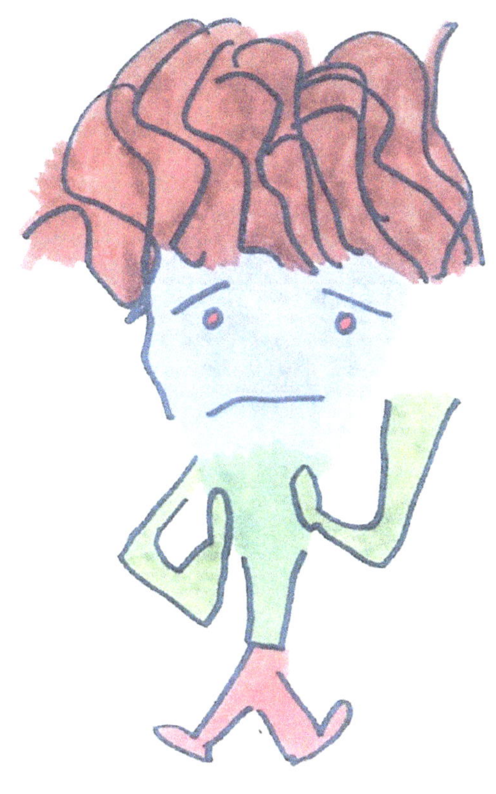

DISAPPOINTED

How healthy it is to love ourselves for our sorrow and
pain and to make of them a forgiven enemy—

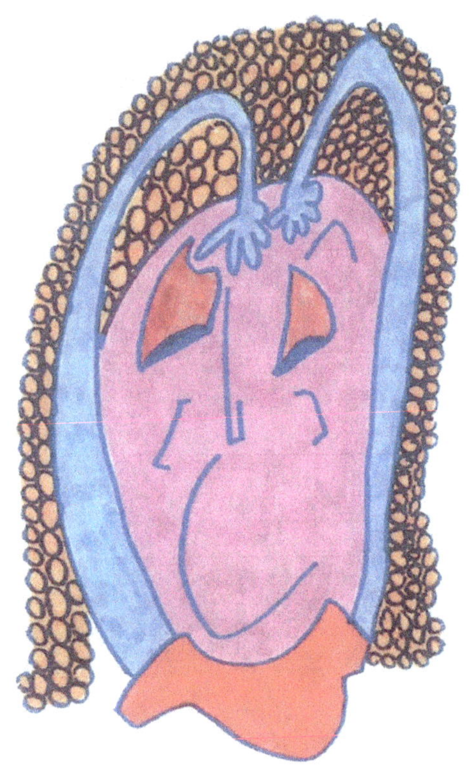

UPLIFTED

to see it—our difficult pain—smiling back at us.

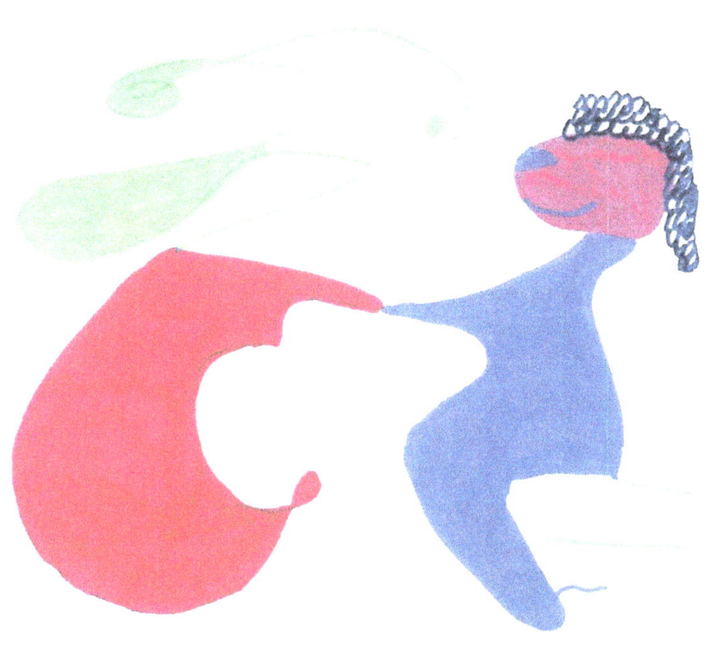

TWO FRIENDS PLAYING

I offer these drawings to you, to delight and gratify—

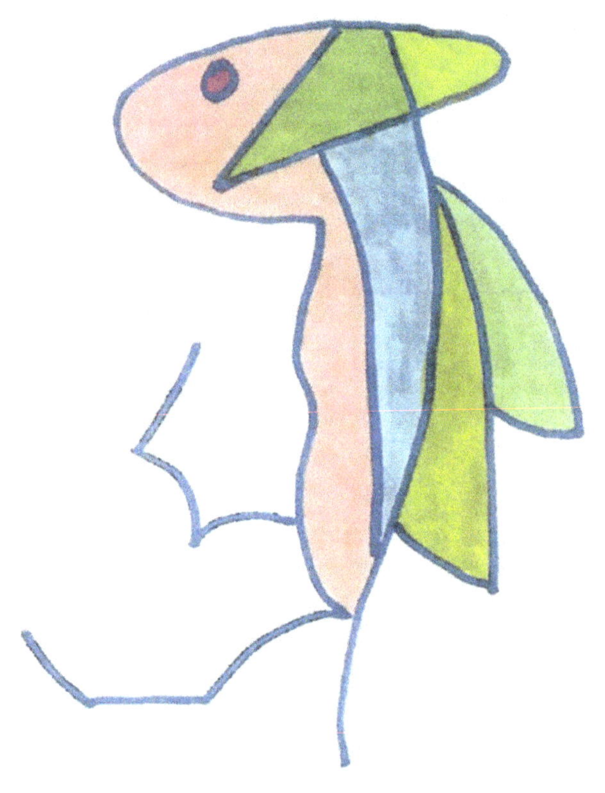

GRASSHOPPER, SITTING

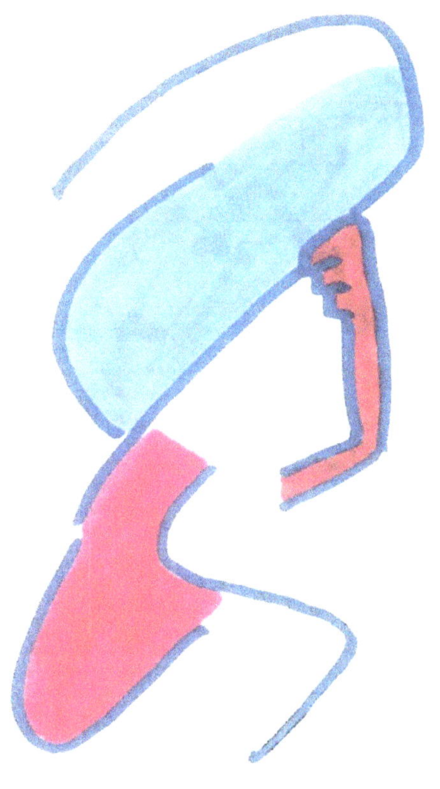

THOUGHTFUL

to make you a bit easier and in dealing with your own,

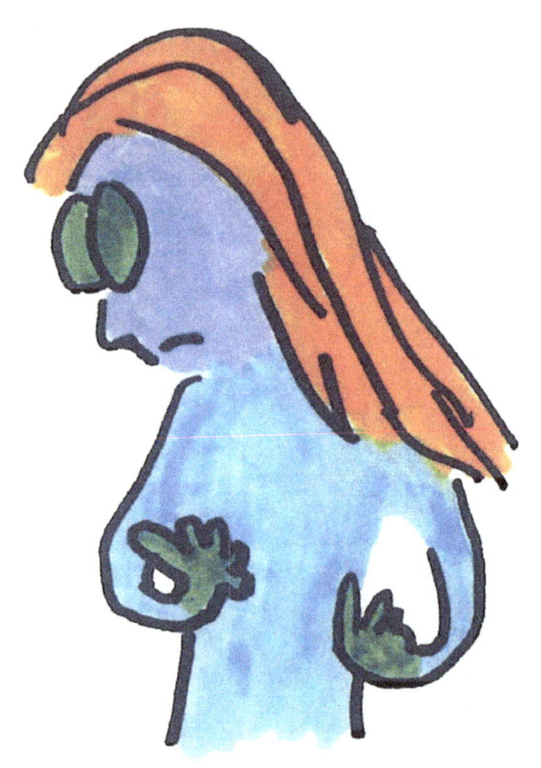

LOSS

perhaps difficult, world.